THE GILL HISTORY OF IRELAND

General Editors: JAMES LYDON, PH.D.
MARGARET MACCURTAIN, PH.D.

IRELAND
BEFORE THE
VIKINGS

Gearóid Mac Niocaill

GILL AND MACMILLAN

First published 1972 by
Gill and Macmillan Ltd
15/17 Eden Quay
Dublin 1
with associated companies in
London, New York, Delhi, Hong Kong,
Johannesburg, Lagos, Melbourne,
Singapore, Tokyo

Second impression 1980

Cover design by Cor Klaasen

7171 0558 X

Printed and bound in Great Britain by
Redwood Burn Limited
Trowbridge & Esher

Contents

Figures in the text

Maps

Foreword

THE study of Irish history has changed greatly in recent decades as more evidence becomes available and new insights are provided by the growing number of historians. It is natural, too, that with each generation new questions should be asked about our past. The time has come for a new large-scale history. It is the aim of the Gill History of Ireland to provide this. This series of studies of Irish history, each written by a specialist, is arranged chronologically. But each volume is intended to stand on its own and no attempt has been made to present a uniform history. Diversity of analysis and interpretation is the aim; a group of young historians have tried to express the view of their generation on our past. It is the hope of the editors that the series will help the reader to appreciate in a new way the rich heritage of Ireland's history.

JAMES LYDON, PH.D.
MARGARET MACCURTAIN, PH.D.

Preface

SINCE the death of Eoin Mac Neill comparatively little work has been done on early Irish political history. The problems of St Patrick's chronology and mission have largely preoccupied the attention of the few concerned with early Irish history: not unnaturally, since they afford splendid opportunities for conjecture and abundant scope for the exercise of academic spleen. The corollary to this activity, however, is that there exists at present no summary of the political history of the period: this is what, in the present essay, I have attempted to provide.

This unashamed stress on politics and power necessarily means that, within the physical limits available, ecclesiastical and literary and artistic affairs are relegated to a minor role. Within the political field itself, many areas and sub-periods are documented only meagrely; and rather than indulge in a recital of rulers of whom nothing is known save their dates of death, if that, I have adopted the thrifty expedient of summarising in diagrams their names, kin, and order of succession, where this is known, showing rulers in italics and the order of succession by a broken line.

Place-names also present something of a problem: many are unidentified, or identified only within very imprecise limits. These I have given in their early form and in italics. A desire to identify these is not mere antiquarianism: the precise location of a battle, for example, may suggest which of the two sides it was that took the offensive, with further implications for policy. Personal names I have given in a standardised form, corresponding to that adopted by M. A. O'Brien in his *Corpus Genealogiarum Hiberniae* (Dublin 1962), omitting minor eccentricities and excepting those few names, such as Patrick, which it would be pedantry to give in any other form.

The bibliography appended is obviously not exhaustive. Eoin Mac Neill and Paul Walsh, to name only the dead, were in the habit, in studies not directly concerned with this period, of harking back to it in passing and tossing out remarks and suggestions which, if this essay were footnoted, would be recorded there. As it is, the bibliography is intended only as a signpost to those who wish to pursue the subject in greater detail.

GEARÓID MAC NIOCAILL

1 The Generations of Chaos

IF the Cunagusos whose ogam stone was erected in
Aghaliskey in east Cork had lived in the seventh century
rather than (perhaps) the fourth, his name would have been
Congus; were he a poet, he would have been, not a *velitas*,
but a *file*; and his sister would have been, not his *swesur*,
but his *siur*: three examples illustrating the fact that between the fourth and the seventh century, Irish underwent
a series of drastic transformations. Of these the chief are
the introduction of lenition, the dropping of final syllables,
the elimination of certain internal syllables, the reduction
of unstressed long vowels, and the reduction of certain
consonant-groups with consequent compensatory length-
ening of short vowels: a formidable list, which in effect
means that the Primitive Irish of the fourth century, by the
time it had evolved into the Old Irish of the seventh
century, was recognisable only with difficulty.

The details and stages of these changes are matters for
the philologist's delight, and may safely be left to him; but
their relevance to the transmission of historical traditions
and institutions is obvious, in that institutions and traditions
existing before and during these changes would necessarily
have to be re-worded and re-interpreted both during them
and when they were completed. Transmission of tradition
was overwhelmingly oral: writing was used only for
memorial (and sometimes boundary) stones, mainly in the
south of the country, and only in the form of ogam, which
was not well adapted for texts of any length. What sur-

vived into the late sixth century survived in the form of a rhythmical syllabic verse, of which the lines were linked by alliteration; and linguistic change must of necessity have entailed modifications in the verse, not necessarily in the direction of more accurate transmission of the contents.

The verse itself seems to represent a very archaic form of oral transmission, of a kind much older than its contents. Many of the institutions of the early Irish period are, like the verse-forms, demonstrably much older, such as the high status attached to the learned class, and the ritual fast used to compel members of certain social classes to fulfil their obligations; others, such as the elaborate system of sureties devised to enforce performance of contracts, basic to the functioning of classical Irish society, are in a large measure developed from more primitive forms. Working back from the classical period – the seventh and eighth centuries – to the obscurities of the early sixth, the fifth and the fourth centuries is therefore a process riddled with traps. The fifth has been very justly described as a 'lost century'; so, *a fortiori,* is all that goes before it. Some few changes of the time stuck in popular memory, because they were on a large scale and enduring; but the cat's-cradle of actions and reactions in which they were embedded, those which contributed to them and those which they in turn triggered off, is, even in the crudest terms, irrecoverable.

Those large-scale changes still recalled, however imprecisely, in the seventh century were the take-over by the Uí Néill of the kingship of Tara, the creation of the states of the Airgialla, the destruction of Emain Macha and overthrow of the Ulaid, the rise of the Eóganacht in Munster, and the penetration of Christianity into the country. What triggered off the political changes can only be guessed at. The possibility of population pressure cannot be ruled out, and much of the overseas expansion of this period may have been an overspill from such pressure. So

Irish colonies make their appearance in Wales: an Irish dynasty established itself in south-west Wales, apparently from the end of the third century, and maintained contact with its homeland, the Déisi and Uí Liatháin in Munster, at least until the eighth century; and there is reason to believe that there were other such settlements on the other side of the Bristol Channel, in Cornwall. Other settlers are found in North Wales at the end of the fourth and beginning of the fifth century: they were of the Laigin, and left their name on the Lleyn peninsula.

The archaic peoples

Dimly perceptible as a background to these events is the existence of a mosaic of peoples of whom few were later to be of any importance. Their names appear in various forms: ending in *-raige* ('the people of'), or as *Dál* ('the share of') or *Corco* (perhaps 'seed') plus a second element, or as a collective noun ending in *-ne*. Some contain animal names, such as Artraige 'bear-people', Osraige 'deer-people', Grecraige 'horse-people', Dartraige 'calf-people', Sordraige 'boar-people'; others, such as the Ciarraige, the Dubraige and Odraige, have a colour (*ciar* 'black', *dub* also 'black', *odor* 'dun') as the first element; others, such as the Cerdraige, seem to have an occupational term as the first element.

All these, when the genealogists got to work in the comparatively Christian atmosphere of the seventh century, were endowed, or endowed themselves, with ancestors whose names included the first element of their names, or had an etymological explanation provided for them, as with the Cerdraige, of whom it was alleged that every man was a craftsman (*cerd*). It seems indisputable, however, that one element in these names is in fact the name or epithet of a divinity which that people had in common – 'the god by whom my people swear', as the law-texts put it. One such people, the Boandraige, have as the first element of

3

their name that of the goddess Boand, who elsewhere appears as the divinised river Boyne; another, the Luigne, contains the name of the god Lug. Whether such a divinity was regarded as being also an ancestor, which would make easier their transformation by the genealogists, is not clear. For that matter, the precise form of their god may not have been too clear to some of these peoples themselves even before the genealogists set to work, if the suggestion that the Bibraige were in fact the 'beaver-people' be correct – since the beaver is not known in Ireland; such a name must derive from a remote continental past.

The rising dynasties who pushed these earlier peoples into the background as a rule described themselves differently: as the Connachta, descendants of Conn, Eóganachta, descendants of Eógan, and even the lesser Cianachta, descendants of Cian, though even they sometimes appear as Dál Cuinn, Dál nEógain and Dál Céin; while still later they merely took their names from an ancestor, real or supposed, in the form favoured by the Uí Néill, the Uí Briúin, the Uí Dúnlainge.

These later terms mean substantially one thing: 'the descendants of X'. They may imply that a more primitive and ill-defined religious bond as a basis for mutual loyalty was being gradually discarded in favour of the more concrete and more easily verifiable ties of blood. If in fact this was the case, it would seem to have been a fairly effective basis of military organisation and recruitment. It is no accident that almost all the earlier -raige and dál peoples are commonly found listed later as aithechtuatha 'subject, tribute-paying peoples'. The only ones to have any later importance were the Dál Fiatach, the Dál nAraide and the Dál Riata in the north, and in the south the Osraige, the Múscraige and the Ciarraige – and even these latter, largely by virtue of alliance to, and support of, the rising Eóganacht dynasty in Munster.

Of the arrival of these latter on the scene in Munster and their displacement of the pre-existing Érainn dynasties, little can be said that is plausible and still less that is certain. Their own origin-legend claimed that the kingship of Cashel was founded by one Conall Corc, son of a British mother, and four or five generations removed from the Eógan from whom the dynasty derived its name, who had returned from a prolonged exile in 'Pictland' (which perhaps meant Britain) to claim the kingship of Munster. Another such legend held that Cashel was founded as a result of a vision seen at Cashel by two swineherds, Duirdriu, swineherd to the king of Éle, and Cuirirán, swineherd to the king of Múscraige, in which an angel recited to them as they slept for three days and three nights the reigns of the kings of Munster. Duirdriu told this to his master, Conall son of Nenta Con, who gave him the land on which he had seen the vision, and in turn Conall Corc bought it from Duirdriu: 'thus the descendants of Duirdriu are entitled to seven *cumal*s from the king of Cashel,' remarks the most primitive version of the tale. In the legend of Conall Corc's exile, only the swineherd of the king of Múscraige is mentioned, and Corc comes to Cashel by chance.

That the dynasty was established in Cashel by Irish colonists returning from Britain, as the legend suggests, is probable enough: the name Cashel itself (*caisel*) is an early borrowing of Latin *castellum*. What prompted the return, if return it was, may be a different story. Conall Corc, if he existed, can hardly have lived earlier than the beginning of the fifth century, which is the date commonly assigned to the expulsion of the rulers of some of the Irish kingdoms established in North Wales: a suggestive coincidence.

The dynasty started, by its own admission, in a small way, on land within the kingdom of Éle. Such scanty and confused evidence as has survived suggests that the man who really put the Eóganacht on their feet in Cashel, and indeed in north Munster, was Óengus son of Nad Fraích, in the second half of the fifth century. Within Munster itself he made little impression on the south, and apparently made no attempt to establish any kind of stronghold there – was very probably in no position to do so, if the legend of his defeat in thirty battles had any basis in fact. The turn in his fortunes was attributed to his recruiting a druid, Boinda, which sorts ill with the legend of his baptism by Patrick.

The chief allies of the Eóganacht in their expansion seem to have been the Corco Óche and the Déisi (which means 'vassalry'), who are credited with having defeated the Uí Fidgenti, an Érainn people, in a number of battles, and with having expelled on behalf of the Eóganacht the Osraige from the area near Cashel and driven them as far east as the river Lingaun, which was to form their historical boundary. Other allies in the rise of the Eóganacht seem to have been recruited from among the Érainn themselves whom the Eóganacht were in process of displacing: such were the Fir Maige, who were settled between the two great Érainn peoples of Uí Liatháin and Uí Fidgenti, making more difficult any concerted action against the Eóganacht. The Corco Baiscind also figure as allies, and were rewarded with land across the Shannon in what is now Clare; this had previously been Connachta territory and was long remembered as such. The seizure of it from the Connachta, however, seems to have been largely the work of a section of the Déisi known later as the Déis Bec (the 'little vassalry') and later again as the Dál gCais. The Múscraige proved even more substantial allies to the Eóganacht, and as a result acquired scattered territories in Munster from the river Brosna in north Tipperary to Loch Léin in the south-west, interwoven with Eóganacht territory 'for the sake of mutual assistance and friendliness.' Of all these changes, however, far-reaching as they were,

6

Fig. 1.

THE EARLY GENERATIONS OF THE EÓGANACHT

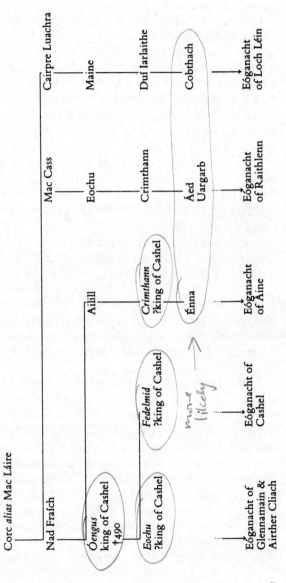

7

the chronology is quite uncertain.

Óengus son of Nad Fraích was reputed to have clashed also with Duí Iarlaithe, his second cousin, who was unwilling to subordinate himself to Óengus. A patched-up truce lasted until Óengus' death (he was slain in 490), whereupon Duí Iarlaithe seized the kingship of Cashel – which at that time was not in practice synonymous with the kingship of Munster. To him are attributed at least two battles which no doubt marked significant stages in the expansion of Eóganacht power southwards and westwards: such, probably, is the undated and unlocated battle of *Findas,* in which Fiachra son of Mac Caille, one of the ancestors of the historical Uí Liatháin, fell. Duí's own death is attributed to a battle with the Uaithne, another Érainn people, at *Áth Cluichir.*

Duí Iarlaithe is counted an ancestor of the Eóganacht of Loch Léin and Irluachair, who were to supply a number of kings of Cashel. As to the three other alleged sons of Corc, none of their descendants held the kingship of Cashel, with the sole exception of Fedelmid son of Tigernach towards the end of the sixth century: he claimed descent from Mac Cass, ancestor of the Eóganacht of Raithlind. The latter's two brothers, Mac Iair and Mac Broc, gave rise to no royal line.

Nothing is known of the length of Duí Iarlaithe's reign, and in some quarters it seems to have been regarded as a usurpation. Indeed, for the first half of the sixth century nothing is known of those who ruled Cashel, save a number of names transmitted by much later regnal lists whose accuracy we have no means of checking. Among those mentioned is Eochaid son of Óengus, ancestor of the Eóganacht of Glennamain (around Glanworth), and his brother Fedelmid, ancestor of the Eóganacht of Cashel; also Crimthann Srem, son of Eochaid, and another Crimthann, son of Fedelmid.

It seems certain that throughout the period the

Eóganacht were throwing out branches. The Eóganacht of west Munster seem to have been the earliest, perhaps including the Eóganacht of Áine (the area around Knockaney in Limerick). The division between the Eóganacht of Glennamain and that of Cashel itself probably came early in the sixth century, and the emergence of the Eóganacht of Airthir Cliach, as an offshoot of the Eóganacht of Glennamain, perhaps a generation later. To Óengus son of Nad Fraích is attributed the establishment of a branch of the Eóganacht in north Clare.

The chaos of these generations in Munster had a counterpart to the north, with the emergence of the Uí Néill.

The emergence of the Uí Néill

The origins of the Uí Néill are impenetrably obscure. They derived their name from their reputed ancestor, Niall Noígiallach ('Niall of the nine hostages'), who lived, if at all, early in the fifth century: he was believed by later tradition to have been a son of Eochu Mugmedon ('lord of slaves'), father of Ailill, Brión and Fiachra, ancestor-figures of the Connachta, and hence Niall's brothers, but – significantly – by a different mother. It has been suggested that Niall's mother was a British slave-girl, which is possible but unprovable.

The rise of the Uí Néill is linked with the destruction of

Fig. 2.

UÍ NÉILL AND CONNACHTA: THE OFFICIAL TRADITION

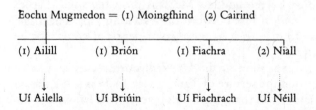

Eochu Mugmedon = (1) Moingfhind   (2) Cairind

(1) Ailill	(1) Brión	(1) Fiachra	(2) Niall
↓	↓	↓	↓
Uí Ailella	Uí Briúin	Uí Fiachrach	Uí Néill

9

the power of the Ulaid, the emergence of the line of states called the Airgialla 'those who give hostages', and the seizure of Tara from the Laigin. The end result was a line of Uí Néill kingdoms which stretched in a crude crescent from the east coast to Sligo Bay in the west and thence northwards to Inishowen. That much is clear. What is far from clear is the sequence in which these changes took place: the more intensely the evidence for them is scrutinised, the more fluid and wraithlike it becomes.

It is eminently possible that the establishment of the Uí Néill in Tara was in some sense a thrust eastwards by the Connachta, an attempt by a younger member of the ruling dynasty, of dubious origin if conjecture about his mother be correct, to acquire sword-land for himself; it is possible that he was encouraged to do so more or less in the words put into the mouth of Muiredach Tírech to the three Collas: 'I see that our children have begun to grow numerous, perhaps they will not be at peace with one another after us. Let each of us part from the other, and do you take in my time one of the lands.' It is possible, if so, that the ruling dynasty of the Connachta assumed that they would be acquiring a subordinate rather than a rival, a relationship somewhat like that claimed much later by the kings of Tara *vis-à-vis* the Airgialla.

All this may have been so, and it is reconcilable with the few texts we possess; but we have no sound means of proving or disproving it, and it would not be beyond a nimble imagination to devise a different scenario. That the sovereignty both of Tara and of Cruachain was personified by the goddess Medb is probably indicative of some kind of link between the two kingships; but if one chose to dismiss it as mere coincidence, it could not be refuted.

The expansion of the Uí Néill northwards may have antedated the seizure of Tara, which there is some reason to believe was changing hands between the Laigin and the

Fig. 3.

THE EARLY GENERATIONS OF THE UÍ NÉILL

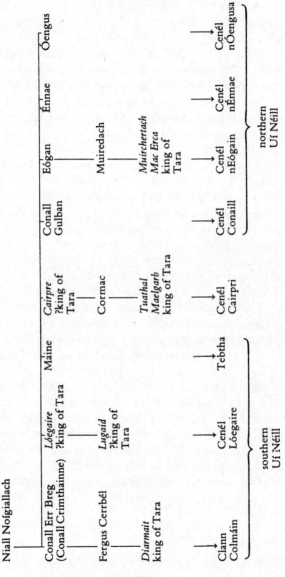

Niall Noígiallach

Conall Err Breg (Conall Crimthainne) — Lóegaire ?king of Tara — Máine — Cairpre ?king of Tara — Conall Gulban — Eógan — Énnae — Óengus

Fergus Cerrbél

Diarmait king of Tara

Lugaid ?king of Tara

Cormac

Muiredach

Tuathal Maelgarb king of Tara

Muirchertach Mac Erca king of Tara

→ Clann Colmáin   → Cenél Lóegaire   → Tebtha   → Cenél Cairpri   → Cenél Conaill   → Cenél nEógain   → Cenél nÉnnae   → Cenél nÓengusa

southern Uí Néill

northern Uí Néill

11

Uí Néill in the late fifth and beginning of the sixth centuries. Niall's alleged son Cairpre left descendants, the Cenél Cairpre, in an area overlapping Longford and Sligo; another, Conall Gulban, left behind rulers of the greater part of Donegal; a third, Eógan, penetrated – at least in the person of his descendants – as far north as Inishowen, which takes its name from him. The southern Uí Néill include the ruling dynasty of Tethba, in a strip to the east of the Shannon and north of the river Inny, which by the late sixth century had extended southwards as far as Durrow; it claimed descent from Maine son of Niall. The ruling dynasty of Meath claimed descent from another son, Conall Err Breg, and yet another, Lóegaire, is credited with founding the minor dynasty of Cenél Lóegaire, a little to the north-west of Tara.

In all, Niall is credited with fourteen sons. In a period when polygyny was acceptable there is nothing remarkable about this, and it is only when one meets such feats of fertility as the thirty-three sons credited to Cathaír Már, allegedly ancestor (probably an ancestor-deity) of the ruling dynasty of the Laigin, that cautious scepticism may yield to incredulity. But it is worth raising the question, even if it is unanswerable, whether all these links with Niall are not perhaps fictitious; whether, indeed, although some recent writers have accepted his existence, and seen in him the first king of Tara of his line, he ever existed at all, and if he did, whether he ever ruled in Tara. If the Uí Néill were really offshoots of the Connachta – and this seems probable – it seems likely also that the foundation of the kingdom of Uisnech, whose focal point is the hill of that name in Westmeath, between Mullingar and Athlone, antedates the foundation of the Uí Néill kingship of Tara.

The Airgialla
The emergence of the Airgialla is hardly less obscure.

Their own origin-legend – a convenience which the Uí Néill lack – attributed to their ancestor figures, the three Collas, the destruction of the power of the Ulaid in seven battles, in the last of which, fought for a day and a night, the Collas unaided drove the Ulaid as far as the valley of the Newry river, which was the later western boundary of the Ulaid. Thereafter they made sword-land of the territory thenceforth occupied by the Airgialla. By definition, pushing back the Ulaid entailed the storming of Emain Macha, the capital of the Ulaid.

In the first six battles, the Collas are said to have had the support of the Connachta, the 'descendants of Conn': in this detail of the legend, at least, it is reasonable to see an echo of the long-standing warfare between the Ulaid and the Connachta which is the background to the *Táin,* the saga of the carrying off of the Bull of Cooley, and which in all probability accounts for the line of defensive earthworks which ran, with gaps, from Sligo to south Armagh: the traditional southern boundary of the Ulaid ran from the river Drowes in the west to the mouth of the Boyne, that is, including the region of Muirtheimne between Carlingford and the Boyne, which was commemorated in later saga as having been in dispute between the Ulaid and their neighbours to the south.

That Connachta here could mean, not exclusively those who later enjoyed that name, but also the incipient Uí Néill, for whom descent from Conn was claimed, is quite probable. But the suggestion that the three Collas should in fact be identified with three of Niall Noígiallach's sons, Conall, Énnae and Eógan, founders of the northern Uí Néill, raises problems. That later genealogical tracts should report that their names were Áed, Cairell and Muiredach is no insuperable objection, since fiction was no stranger to these compilations. What is implausible is that these sons should, having thrust into Ulidia and made swordland of it, thereupon abandon it, good land though much of it was, for the poor country of Inishowen and Donegal. That the Airgialla at a later date were in some ill-defined degree subordinate to the Uí Néill king of Tara carries little weight: such relationships could arise in many ways.

We are left, then, with two possibilities: that the Uí Néill defeated the Ulaid, but left the land to its pre-existing inhabitants, who were to crystallise into the Airgialla of historic times, with some kind of assurance against the return of the Ulaid; or secondly that the Ulaid were in fact defeated by the ancestors of the historic Airgialla, who were (at least in part) intruders from outside the territory ruled by the Ulaid. Against the first view is the fact that the origin-legend of the Airgialla, though viewing matters from an Uí Néill standpoint, making the three Collas offshoots of the Uí Néill ancestral line almost on the same level as the Connachta, and representing their conquest of the territory of the Ulaid as having been suggested by Muiredach Tírech, reputed grandfather of Niall, because the Ulaid were 'undutiful' towards him, does not suggest that the Uí Néill had any part in the conquest save in the persons of the three Collas themselves.

The alternative is that the Airgialla may have been in origin peoples forced against the Ulaid by pressure from the incipient Uí Néill dynasty behind them. A glance at a map* will show, in the historic period, in the north-east of the country, the Dál Fiatach, the Dál nAraide and the Dál Riata, encircled from the north coast almost completely to the east coast by a layer of Airgialla kingdoms, and the Airgialla in turn ringed by various branches of the Uí Néill, which were still, in the eighth and ninth centuries, exerting pressure on the Airgialla. Such pressure would, in part at least, have given an impulse to the spread of the Dál Riata overseas to Scotland about the end of the fifth century.

The actual date of the overthrow, as symbolised by the

*See page 38.

14

storming of Emain, was by later tradition very variously calculated. The origin-legend of the Airgialla would put it not later than the beginning of the fifth century. The suggestion that it must have occurred much later, after Patrick had established his missionary headquarters at Armagh, two miles to the east of Emain, depends largely on the premise that Emain was regarded as the capital of the chief, and probably most powerful, Irish kingdom in the first half of the fifth century, or he would not have established himself there. It is true that this was common missionary procedure at the time, but the argument perhaps assumes a wider and more accurate knowledge of what must have been a very fluid political situation, and indeed of Irish geography, than Patrick probably possessed. One might equally well assume that Patrick established himself near Emain because it was the seat of kingship best known to him – if only by report. In short, on the available evidence, the date of the destruction of Emain presents an insoluble problem.

Uí Néill and Laigin

The kingship of Tara itself in the fifth and sixth centuries presents similar problems. Uí Néill tradition held it to have been possessed by them to the exclusion of all others; but the claim is contested by the tribal histories of the Laigin, who claim it for Bresal Bélach (whose death is assigned to the year 435, for what this is worth), Muiredach Sníthe, of the same generation as Bresal Bélach, Móenach son of Cairthenn, perhaps the Cairthenn Muach who appears as an ancestor of the Uí Máil, and lastly one Nad-Buidb son of Ercc Buadach of the Uí Dega. In this the tradition of the Laigin may well reflect the actual to-and-fro of possession of Tara at the time.

Later tradition assigned, as was its wont, a precise chronology to the high points in the struggle between the Laigin and the Uí Néill, that is, the pitched battles. There is no reason to suppose such dates to be accurate, but the sequence of battles is in all probability correct. On this warfare was later superimposed, not earlier than the eighth century, a tradition of a tribute, the *bórama,* payable by the Laigin to the kings of Tara – as a rule, unwillingly. With the passage of time the tribute swelled, so that by the time the tradition reached the eleventh century the amount payable had reached fantastic proportions. The tale may in fact be securely dismissed as pure fiction, devised to legitimise Uí Néill aggression against the Laigin retrospectively; it has no place in the history of the fifth and sixth centuries.

Among the earliest battles in this conflict, if we set aside the tales of battles by Bresal Bélach and Labraid and the slaying of Niall Noígiallach by Eochaid son of Énnae, is the great slaughter of the Laigin set down under the year 452, and their rout in the following year by Lóegaire son of Niall Noígiallach. This was believed to have been at the beginning of his reign, since in the following year he is alleged to have held his inauguration rite, the 'mating' of Tara. Four years or so later, in 458/9, he was defeated by the Laigin in the battle of *Áth Dara,* near Maganey on the Barrow, a position which implies that Lóegaire was the attacker; three years later, he died, and was buried, it was believed, at the hill of Tara, standing upright and facing the Laigin to the south.

He seems to have been followed as king of Tara by Ailill Molt, who also figures as king of Connacht. Whether in fact Ailill should be counted as his immediate successor *de facto* depends perhaps on whether he had physical possession of Tara at the time: it may have changed hands a number of times in this period, situated as it is within easy striking distance of the later historical boundary of the Laigin. The tradition of Laginian kings of Tara at this period certainly implies something of the kind, and the 'feast' of Tara, the inauguration rite of the new king, was not believed to have been held by Ailill for at least five years after the death of Lóegaire, in 467. This was followed a year later, somewhat embarrassingly, by a defeat at the hands of the Laigin at *Duma Aichir,* somewhere in the territory of the Laigin: a defeat which was partly redeemed by a victory over them at Croghan Hill in Offaly in 475.

It seems not impossible that Ailill's misfortunes were in part due to a less than wholehearted support by the Uí Néill. The sons and grandsons of Niall may well have resented him as an outsider, attempting to take over their hard-won territory; and in 482 Lugaid son of Lóegaire and Muiredach son of Eógan combined to defeat Ailill in the battle of Faughan Hill, near Kells. Fergus Cerrbél, Fiachra Lond, king of the Dál nAraide, and Crimthand king of the Laigin, are also reputed to have taken part in the battle against Ailill: a remarkable combination, if true.

Ailill's death at Faughan marks the end of intervention by the Connachta in the affairs of the Uí Néill, but not of the conflict between the Laigin and the Uí Néill. In 485 Finnchad, king of the Laigin, fell to the Uí Néill under either Cairpre son of Niall or Muirchertach Mac Erca at Granard in Longford, following a thrust northward by the Laigin.

The Laigin, with admirable persistence, carried the fight to the Uí Néill again in 494, when they were defeated at Teltown in Meath by Cairpre son of Niall, and again in 499, when they suffered defeat, again at Cairpre's hands, by Lough Slevin in Westmeath. Following up his advantage, Cairpre struck southwards in 501 and inflicted a defeat on the Laigin at *Cenn Ailbe* in south Kildare.

This run of good fortune for the Uí Néill lapsed in 503 with their defeat by the Laigin in the battle of *Druim Lóchmaige,* which was repeated in 507 in the battle of *Ard Corann,* in which Lugaid son of Lóegaire fell. In 510 Failge Berraide, who seems to have been an early ruler of what was later to be the Uí Failge, drove north into Uí Néill territory and defeated Fiacha son of Niall at Frevin Hill, to the west of Lough Owel in Westmeath. This series of humiliations ended in 516, when Fiacha defeated Failge at *Druim Derg,* which is unidentified, but was probably in Laginian territory. The defeat seems to have been decisive: from it later tradition, probably rightly, dated the final loss to the Laigin of the rich plains of Westmeath.

The struggle within the Uí Néill

For some years after the battle of *Druim Derg,* there is no record of conflict between the Laigin and the Uí Néill. These latter, and probably also the former, may have been preoccupied with internal disputes: in 520 Ardgal son of Conall Cremthainne was defeated and slain in the battle of *Détnae* in Brega by Muirchertach Mac Erca of the northern Uí Néill, with the support of Colgu, king of the Airgiallan kingdom of Airthir. From this battle probably dates the supremacy of Muirchertach among the Uí Néill; and to set the seal on his position, he inflicted in 528 two defeats on the Laigin, the first probably at Kineagh in north Kildare, and the second at Assey in Meath, countering the Laigin reaction to the first. Neither is distinguished by any eminent casualties, and both in effect were hardly more than raids. In 534 Muirchertach died: a death which became encrusted with legend, which picturesquely depicts it as being carried out by drowning (in a vat of wine), burning and piercing with a spear.

His successor was Tuathal Maelgarb, grandson of Cairpre, who met with some unexplained opposition from the Cianachta of Brega; he defeated them in 535 at Logher, in Meath. Later tradition credits him with little else: the removal of a possible rival, Mac Erca son of Ailill Molt, was the work of the Laigin, who slew him in a battle at *Tortu* near Ardbraccan in 543; any possible threat from the main body of the Connachta was met by the northern Uí Néill under Forgus and Domnall, two sons of Muirchertach Mac Erca, and Ainmire and Nainnid, two sons of Sétna, who in the same year clashed with, and slew, Eógan Bél, king of Connacht, at Sligo. Tuathal himself seems to have taken no part in these events, and was removed in 544 by one Máel Mór son of Airgetán, allegedly a uterine brother of Diarmait son of Fergus Cerrbél; it is very probable that Diarmait himself was the instigator of the killing, but since Máel Mór himself was killed on the spot, no proof was possible. Diarmait at least profited by it, and succeeded to the kingship of Tara, though not without some difficulty.

The Laigin in the fifth-sixth centuries

The surviving evidence, scanty though it is, suggests a period of extreme confusion among the Laigin in the 5th–6th centuries, with the kingship, or at least the chief power, oscillating from line to line. Among those listed as kings of the Laigin are Crimthann, son of Énnae Cennselach, whose death is dated in 483 and 486; he is reputedly the ancestor of the later ruling dynasty of the Laigin. Another is Findchad, who was slain in 485, and belonged to the Uí Garrchon, later regarded as one of the fortuatha 'outside peoples' of the Laigin; his son, Fróech, also figures as king of the Laigin, and was overthrown in 493 by one Eochu son of Cairpre. These were followed by Illann and Ailill, two sons of Dúnlang, reputedly first cousin of Énnae Cennselach.

Illann's death is dated in 527; elsewhere, however, he is accounted a contemporary of the fifth-century Lóegaire son of Niall, king of Tara. The remainder of the sixth century is filled up with four descendants of Ailill in succession: Cormac son of Ailill, Cairpre son of Cormac, Colmán Mór son of Cairpre, and Áed Cerr son of Cairpre. The last is not elsewhere accounted a descendant of Ailill, but is attached – with much greater probability – to the Uí Máil.

Fig. 4.

INTERRELATIONSHIPS OF THE LAIGIN
according to Laigin tradition

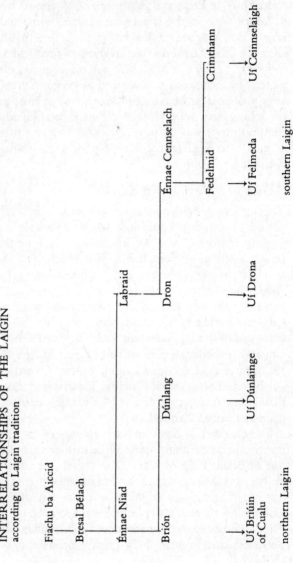

Fiachu ba Aiccid

Bresal Bélach

Énnae Niad — Labraid

Brión — Dúnlang — Dron — Énnae Cennselach — Fedelmid / Crimthann

Uí Briúin of Cualu →

Uí Dúnlainge →

Uí Drona →

Uí Felmeda →

Uí Ceinnselaig →

northern Laigin   southern Laigin

In effect, all this is a combination of fiction and guess-work, concocted by early historians to fill in the void in later knowledge of these decades in the history of the Laigin. It is entirely possible that some of these names are genuinely those of persons predominant among the Laigin in the period in which they were being pressed out of Meath by the Uí Néill, as may also be that of Nad Buidb son of Ercc Buadach, reputedly a grand-nephew of Énnae Cennselach, of the unimportant people of Uí Dega, accounted in some sources the last king of Tara of the Laigin. Of them all, Áed Cerr is likely to be the most genuinely historical, and his death is dated, somewhat shakily, in the last decade of the sixth century.

The Connachta

The rulers of the Connachta in these centuries are as shadowy as those of the Laigin. Later theory held them to be the stock of Eochu Mugmedon, but there is much confusion over the kinship groups to which the putative kings of the Connachta belonged. Nath Í, assigned to the early fifth century, was believed to be a son of Fiachra, from whom the Uí Fiachrach claimed descent, but a certain Amalgaid, from whom Tirawley is named, is also found drifting in this obscurity, also a son of Fiachra, and with some claim to be regarded as king of the Connachta. He was succeeded, it was believed, by his nephew Ailill Molt son of Nath Í, who was killed in the battle of Faughan Hill in 482. We may accept that Ailill was also king of Tara: so seventh-century Uí Néill tradition held, and on this point it is unlikely to be wrong. He was succeeded in Connacht by Duí Galach, son of Brión, eponymous ancestor of the later Uí Briúin dynasty. It is possible that while Ailill Molt, and the branch of the Connachta he headed, were trying to consolidate their rule in Tara, the section headed by Duí Galach had been able to establish a basis of power in the west. The death of Ailill's son, Mac

Erca, in Uí Néill territory in 543 suggests the possibility that his branch of the Connachta still had their eye on territory east of the Shannon.

Duí Galach's death as king of Connacht is assigned to the year 502. His successor, Eógan Bél, belonged in all probability to the Uí Fiachrach, as probably did the next king, Ailill Inbanda, who died in 550. The pattern of oscillation between these two branches of the Connachta, then, had begun by the middle of the sixth century.

The introduction of Christianity

The introduction of Christianity into the country is obscure both in chronology and channels. From an early date it seems to have been diffusing into Ireland from Britain, and the vocabulary of this new religion was borrowed either from British or from Latin pronounced in the British fashion – such terms as *cáisc* 'Easter', *cruimthir* 'priest', *caille* 'veil', *fescor* 'vespers' and *sléchtad* 'prostration, bowing down', made their way into primitive Irish no later than the fifth century, before it evolved into archaic Old Irish. British slaves captured in raids are one possible channel of entry, and contacts mediated by the Irish colonies in Britain are another. From at least the early fifth century Christians were to be found in the south of the country, and were known, at least by report, to the church in Gaul. They formed the 'Irish believing in Christ' to whom in 431 the deacon Palladius was sent. Of the fate of his mission nothing is known.

Of the other missionaries, who looked rather to the church in Britain than to the church in Gaul, a little more is known. The most celebrated at a later date was Patrick, whose activity is probably to be dated to the second half of the fifth century. The date of death, 493, assigned to him by later annalists may well be more or less correct. His work seems mainly to have lain in the area later occupied by the kingdoms of Airthir and the Ulaid; and he is the

EARLY EVANGELISING
ACTIVITY

PATRICK

TIGERNACH

SECUNDINUS

AUXILIUS

CIARAN²

CIARAN¹

AILBE

DECLAN

0   80Kms
0   50MIs

only one of these missionaries to have left any documentary
account of his mission, in his *Confession* and *Epistle to
Coroticus* – neither of them intended as historical accounts,
but rather in the first case an apologia for his work, and
in the second a rebuke to a king who had carried off some
of Patrick's converts. Other missionaries, whom later
legend represents as subordinates of Patrick, in reality
probably worked independently: Secundinus, alias Sechnaill, worked south of Patrick, in Meath, where one of his

foundations, Dunshaughlin (*Domnach Sechnaill*), preserves his name; another, Auxilius, left a foundation at Killashee (*Cell Ausaile*) near Naas in Kildare.

Other missionary activity was carried on among the Osraige by Ciarán, founder of the monastery of Seirkieran, in the late fifth and early sixth century. Of approximately the same period, Ailbe seems to have been active in north Munster, and his death is attributed to the year 527. A seeming contemporary of Ailbe, Declán, was active among the Déisi of Munster. In the land bordering the Shannon another Ciarán, founder of Clonmacnois, was active during a brief life: he died, aged thirty-three, in 549; and further north, among the Airgialla, Tigernach, founder of Clones, who died in 549/50.

British influence remained constant throughout: from *Candida Casa*, at Whitern on the northern shore of the Solway, founded by Ninian early in the fifth century, where Enda of Aran, Tigernach of Clones, Eógan of Ardstraw, Finnian of Moville, and Cairpre of Coleraine are reputed to have studied; from the apocalyptic Gildas, who is alleged to have visited Ireland in the seventh decade of the sixth century; and most of all, from David (†589) in Menevia, who counted among his disciples such Irish churchmen as Máedóc of Ferns (†626), Scuithín of Slieve Margy near Carlow, and Modomnóc of Tibragny in Kilkenny, while others, such as Finnian of Clonard (†549), Senán of Scattery Island, Findbarr of Cork and Brendan of Clonfert (†577) were reputed to have visited him. Finnian himself was the founder of a notable monastery, largely under the influence of Cadoc, founder of Llangarvan, and of Gildas, with whom he corresponded on points of monastic discipline. In this he is characteristic: the British influence bore mainly on details of monastic organisation and discipline and the forms of the liturgy.

The later lives of these saints show them as thaumaturges much in contact with kings at various levels. In this latter point they may well be correct, since a fixed principle in classical Irish law, and doubtless in pre-classical law, was that for a kinless man (a 'headless man' – *dícenn* – is the Irish term) the king of the *tuath* was responsible; equally, it was standard missionary policy to aim for the top ranks of the society being evangelised. Thus both legal custom and missionary policy may well have assisted the spread of Christianity: this, and the forceful character of the missionaries, for the paganism which it was intended to displace was not itself aggressive nor prone to seek converts. It had rather the tolerance of other gods characteristic of polytheism. Not that much is known about early Irish paganism with any degree of certainty. Animals, including those hunted, figured largely in it, and divinities attached to such natural features as rivers – the Boyne, for example, appears as a divinity (*Boand*). Fertility cults seem to have been widespread, and the pagan year hinged on four festivals, *Imbolc* (1 February), *Beltaine* (1 May), *Lugnasad* (1 August) and *Samhain* (1 November) of which the first and the last proved susceptible of a take-over as Christian festivals. Columcille is credited with a bid to take over the harvest-festival of *Lugnasad* by converting it into a 'Feast of the Ploughmen', not apparently with any great success.

The introduction of Christianity in the long run affected the structure of Irish society. The establishment of communities of men separated from their kin, perhaps also from their native *tuath* in the 'white martyrdom' of which an eighth-century Irish homily speaks, posed problems; so too did the emergence of a set of 'druids' with a new, Latin, learning, parallel to those who had hitherto been the custodians of learning, whether historical tradition or law or poetry. The solution eventually proved to be that of assigning such dignitaries as bishops the same status as the king of the *tuath,* and less exalted churchmen a proportionate status; but this assimilation was not achieved before the middle of the sixth century, when Christianity had waxed too strong to be ignored, and had acquired a well-developed organisation with well-defined spheres of jurisdiction.

Instant evangelisation is of course a myth of later ecclesiastical saga: Diarmait son of Fergus Cerrbél, king of Tara in the mid-sixth century, was almost certainly a pagan – and perhaps some sort of Christian also, in the pattern exemplified much later in Iceland, paying obeisance to the Christian god when life was quiet and undisturbed, but in times of stress calling on the gods of his ancestors. Similarly with his contemporary, Eógan Bél, king of the Connachta; and the case was probably very common. Equally common must have been families of mixed beliefs. Ailill, son of Dúnlang, reputed king of the Laigin in the early sixth century, was believed to have had two daughters, Mugain and Fedelm, who adopted Christianity as virgins and, almost inevitably, were later numbered among the saints; so also his son Cormac had two, Ethne and Dar Cárthaind; and in turn, Cormac's son Cairpre bestowed two daughters, Cuimne and Sodelb, on the church. All these daughters, in fact, were later commemorated as saints; and it is probable that these later commemorations were right in so doing, insofar as Christians at the time were comparatively few in number and to break with the cult transmitted by one's forefathers took some courage, at least moral. It is indeed possible that it was often more convenient for a pagan father at this period, if he had a surplus of daughters, to allow them to take the veil as Christians than to marry them off, with the attendant bother of ensuring that the prospective husband was of suitable rank and had an attractive bride-price to offer – against which, however, the dowry would have to be offset. Some such daughters, indeed, may have been of dubious origin, such as Brigit of Kildare, whose father was of noble blood, but whose mother was a slave-girl.

By the mid-sixth century, Christianity was some distance

from being integrated into society. Early legislation assumes that Christians are in a minority, and should treat the surrounding society with some reserve. Disputes between Christians should be settled among themselves, rather than by recourse to the professional jurisconsults, who were presumed to be pagans, and probably, since the caste of jurists had not yet hived off from the old druidic caste, druids also. Alms offered to the church by pagans are to be refused. In contrast to the surrounding society, monogamy is enforced, even where a wife proves barren, which pagan society regarded as a disaster to be remedied by taking another wife.

Authority among these Christians was wielded, not by abbots, as later, but by bishops, each with his own defined area of jurisdiction, usually co-extensive with the *tuath*. He might exercise no functions in the jurisdiction of another bishop without the permission of this latter, nor might any cleric minister within a bishop's *paruchia* (diocese) without permission. The clergy were of various origins, distinguishing themselves from the pagans by shaven heads and wearing tunics: some were of noble blood, some had been slaves; and they were permitted to remain married, but to one wife only.

2 The Geography of Politics before 600

BY the second half of the sixth century the outlines of later political geography are becoming visible. Not that the limits of any particular *tuath* can be defined with any great precision, save where they coincide with some natural boundary such as a river or mountain range: the picture is, unavoidably, impressionistic.

The *tuath* is the basic political unit. The word itself means, basically, 'a people': it cannot be defined in terms of territorial extent or population, and the best approximation to a definition is a group of people sufficiently large to be ruled by a king, and conscious of their otherness from neighbouring groups. If they thought of themselves as a *tuath,* and if their neighbours thought of them as a *tuath,* they were. The definition is circular, and in the case of so basic a unit can hardly be otherwise. The bond between the kindreds of the *tuath* was not one of common descent, genuine or imaginary: the unimportant Uí Téig, settled around the north-east shoulder of the Wicklow mountains, recognised over a dozen kindreds within the *tuath,* of diverse origins. Their bond was their common rule by a king.

Similarly within the larger units: in each of the major political regions a ruling dynasty had, by the second half of the sixth century, established itself, with a number of offshoots of itself, and a number of satellites around it. Each such dynasty and its offshoots claimed descent from a common ancestor, and a *tuath* whose rulers could not claim such descent was described as a *fortuath,* which may best be translated as 'outsiders', though indeed many such may well have been settled in the area before the emergence of those who so described them. In some cases, descent may have been inferred from status, and a genealogy cooked up to fit the political facts: such are the Uí Failgi, who emerge at the end of the sixth century, and by virtue of their political importance find themselves in due course credited with descent from Catháir Már, from whom the Laigin ruling dynasty claimed descent. All others in the territory of the Laigin were at best *fortuatha.* In Munster, those who could not claim descent from Ailill Ólom, such as the various Érainn peoples whom the Eóganacht had displaced, ranked as *fortuatha;* the Uí Néill and the Connachta, claiming descent from Conn, excluded from their charmed circle such peoples as the Luigne, the Delbna, the Gailenga and the Cianachta.

Political subordination

Within these greater units were various degrees of subordination. The king of a single *tuath* was the lowest level of king: the equivalent, in political terms, of the self-sufficient farmer within the *tuath.* Inevitably, such a king, like his own commoners, found it expedient to enter into a subordinate relationship to another more powerful than he. It was, like clientship, entirely a personal relationship, and the over-king to whom the king of a *tuath* submitted acquired thereby no personal connection with the men of the latter's *tuath:* anything they found themselves obliged to do as a result of their king's submission was done by virtue of their subordination to their own king, not on the orders of the over-king. Such subordination was pyramidal in form: the king who was over-king of another *tuath* was expected to have at least two *tuaths* as well as his own subordinate to him. Above such an over-king was the king of a province – of the Laigin, or Connachta, or Cashel.

Such was the theory: the reality was likely to be less tidy.

The submission of the subordinate king was accomplished by his 'going into the house' of the over-king, as the phrase was, and accepting from the superior king a gift which is sometimes designated by the same term (*rath*) as the 'fief' given to a client, and at other times described, significantly, as 'protection' (*cumtach*). The acceptance of this gift obliged the recipient to render various duties to the over-king, the most important of which were to take part with his hosting in any campaign to which the over-king summoned him, and to render him tribute – which itself was naturally supplied by the members of the subordinate *tuath*, but for whose render the king himself was personally responsible. The subordination could be guaranteed, and usually was, by hostages given to the over-king.

The incidents of subordination varied, doubtless, from place to place, and their nature is clearer from the exemptions of which we occasionally have note than from anything else. Thus, the seven divisions of the Laígis, subordinate to the king of the Laigin, owed him hosting, but no more than twenty-one fighting men from each of the seven divisions, plus their king and two personal servitors; which we may contrast with the seven hundred fighting men claimable, in theory, from the king of a subordinate *tuath*. Their king himself was claimed to be exempt from the duty of supplying malt and food to the king of the Laigin, and to owe only seven beasts, to be delivered on hoof, when the king of Laigin was moving against Munster. They were not bound to pay a *cumal* for every man killed in their country – which is precisely the amount to which his maternal kin could lay claim in that event – nor to contribute cattle as provender for hostings. These immunities were allegedly in consideration of good service against the men of Munster in the remote past;

and another *fortuath,* the Fothairt, were claimed to enjoy similar immunities.

On a wider scale, something is known of the relationships alleged to exist between the king of Cashel and the other kingdoms of Munster, although, as in the case of the Laígis and Fothairt, the text supplying our information is by no means as early as the late sixth century. The various branches of the Eóganacht, of course, received no 'fief' or 'protection', nor were they liable for tribute. Of the non-Eóganacht kingdoms, the Uí Liatháin ranked first, with the dubious privilege of not supplying hostages to the king of Cashel until all the other kingdoms had done so. As 'fief', their king was entitled to 30 *cumals* every seven years – the same period as in ordinary clientship. The king of the Déisi was entitled to 50 *cumals,* and the king of Fir Maige to 20. There is no record of other 'fiefs': the Múscraige and Éile and Uí Fidgenti apparently enjoyed exemption from this particular type of subordination, and the king of the Múscraige was held to be of equal rank not only with the king of Uí Fidgenti, but also with the kings of the Eóganacht of Irluachair and the Eóganacht of Raithlenn, to whom, however, he would have to yield precedence. The king of the Múscraige, moreover, was entitled to a cow from every prey taken by the king of Cashel, and his wife was entitled to have three of her women in the retinue of the queen of Cashel. Such posts of honour are found allotted to other kingdoms: the Fir Maige were entitled to have a man as confidant of the king of Cashel, the Déise were to supply a jurisconsult, the Múscraige a man of letters. The position of the Osraige *vis-à-vis* the king of Cashel was ticklish: they were of Munster and yet not of it, and the text which furnishes these details notes that on a hosting their king accompanies the king of Cashel, that he may come to Cashel with a retinue of nine, the number appropriate to a king on private business, thus underlining the fact that he was not really subordinate to the king of Cashel, receiving no 'fief' and rendering no tribute; and that he ranks with the king of Éile (though where this latter stands is not clear), unless the king of Laigin be present to outrank him.

Treaty relationships

Vertical relationships of this kind are universal in early Irish society and politics. Between one kingdom and another, where no such subordination existed, relationships varied widely both from place to place and from reign to reign. Each *tuath* is an entity in itself: its members have obligations to one another, but not to outsiders, to men of another *tuath*. A member of one *tuath* has no rights in another *tuath*. This lack of rights, however, is mitigated by a number of devices. The member of a *tuath* seeking to prosecute a blood-feud against a member of another *tuath* was left on the whole to his own devices, and at his own risk. But it could happen that two such neighbouring territories concluded a treaty of numerous possible degrees of complexity: at its simplest it amounted to a treaty of peace and non-aggression, but it could extend to arrangements for mutual enforcement of legal claims, which could accommodate claims for homicide. It was entered into entirely at the discretion of the king of the *tuath*, but to be made binding, since it affected every member of the *tuath*, it had to be formally proclaimed at an *óenach*.

Enforcement of such a treaty depended as a rule on the appointment of one or more hostage-sureties (*aitire*) on each side. In case of a breach of the treaty, the *aitire* surrendered himself to the king of the aggrieved *tuath,* who kept him in custody for a defined period, usually ten days, during which the king of the offending *tuath* was expected to ransom him for his full 'body-price' or wergild of seven *cumals*. Otherwise, the *aitire* could, at the end of his period of 'captivity', ransom himself and satisfy whatever claim was outstanding from his own property, thereby rendering his own king liable for very heavy compensation, covering both the ransom and twice the amount of the original claim, and compensation for loss of time and labour while in 'captivity'.

★   ★   ★

These, then, being the relations between states, what, in concrete terms, were the states in question?

The kingdom of Cashel

The most powerful kingdom in the second half of the sixth century, considered in terms of wealth rather than vigour, is Munster, ruled ultimately from Cashel by the Eóganacht, who naturally form a settlement around Cashel itself. There are however other branches of the ruling family scattered through the province: the Eóganacht of Raithlenn in the Lee and Bride valleys to the west of Cork harbour, the Eóganacht of Irluachair around Lough Leane in Kerry, the Eóganacht of Glennamain around Glanworth in the north Cork lowlands, and the Eóganacht of Áine, around Knockany in Limerick, with yet another, though very minor, branch in the north of Clare. These occupied much of the best land in Munster.

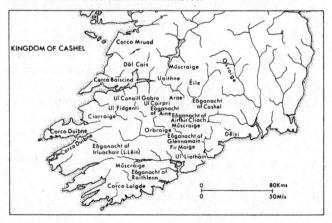

In the uplands to the north and north-west of Cashel the Éile predominated, with a branch of the Múscraige to the west, between the Éile and Loch Derg. To the south of these latter were the Uaithne; over the Shannon, and physically much more a part of Connacht, lay the Dál gCais, with the Corco Mruad (in Burren) and the Corco Baiscinn at their northern and southern westerly extremities respectively. To the south-east of Cashel, in the lowlands beyond the Suir, lay the Déisi; west of these, over the Blackwater and in the alternating ridges and depressions of east Cork, were the Érainn people of the Uí Liatháin, to the west of whom again lay yet another branch of the Múscraige, forming something of a buffer between the Eóganacht of Glennamain to their north and the Corco Loígde to the south and south-west. These latter largely occupied the south-western sea-coast, with in the extreme west the Corco Duibne, who were flanked along the Shannon estuary and in the uplands of north Kerry by the Ciarraige. To the east of these latter, in the Limerick lowlands, were the Uí Fidgenti, to whose north, by the Shannon, were the Uí Conaill Gabra, along the Maigue to their east the Uí Cairpre, and the Orbraige in the uplands to the south. Sandwiched in between these and the Eóganacht of Cashel were the Arae to the north, the Eóganacht of Cashel and yet another branch of the Múscraige.

It is notable that throughout the province the Eóganacht or their allies form barriers between the Érainn peoples. Thus the Eóganacht of Raithlenn form a barrier between the Uí Liatháin and the Corco Laígde; the Eóganacht of Loch Léin bar the way between the Ciarraige and the Corco Loígde; between the Uí Fidgenti and the Uí Liatháin lie the Eóganacht of Glennamain and their allies the Fir Maige; while the Dál gCais block any linkage of the Uí Fidgenti with the Connachta.

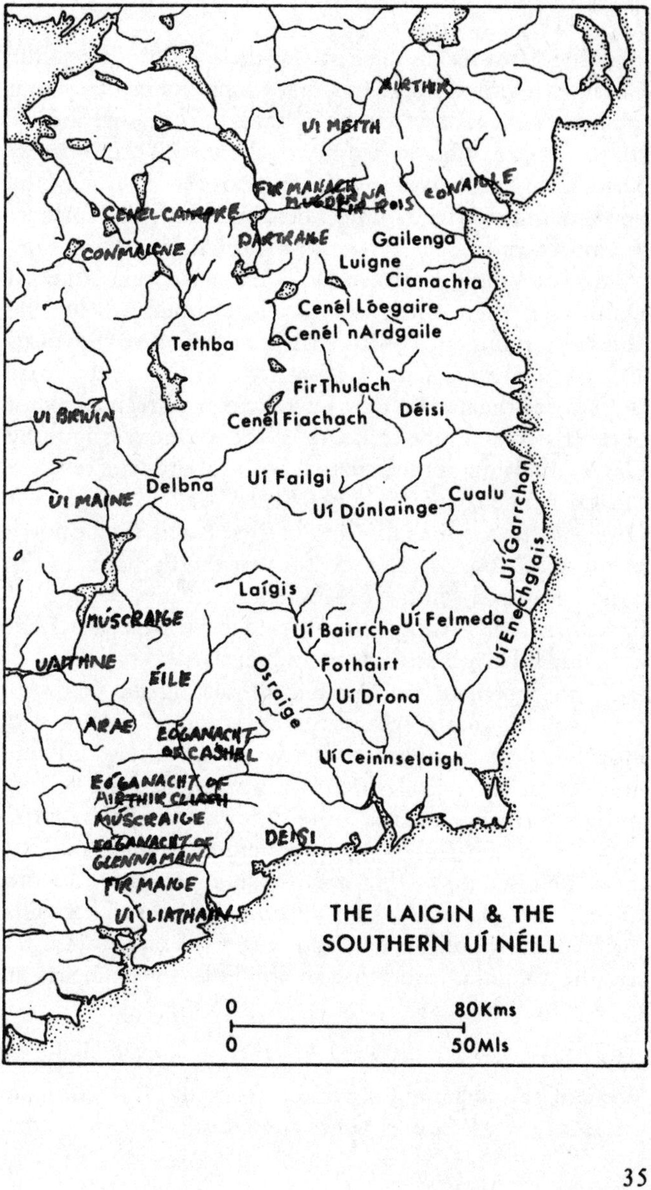
AIRTHIR
UI MEITH
FIR MANACH
MUGDORNA
FIR ROIS
CONAILLE
CENEL CAIRPRE
DARTRAIGE
CONMAICNE
Gailenga
Luigne
Cianachta
Cenél Lóegaire
Cenél nArdgaile
Tethba
Fir Thulach
UI BRIUIN
Cenél Fiachach
Déisi
Uí Failgi
Delbna
UI MAINE
Uí Dúnlainge
Cualu
Uí Garrchon
Uí Enechglais
Laígis
MÚSCRAIGE
Uí Bairrche
Uí Felmeda
UAITHNE
Osraige
Fothairt
ÉILE
Uí Drona
ARAE
EÓGANACHT OF CASHEL
Uí Ceinnselaigh
EÓGANACHT OF AIRTHIR CLIACH
MÚSCRAIGE
DÉISI
EÓGANACHT OF GLENNAMAIN
FIR MAIGE
UÍ LIATHAIN
THE LAIGIN & THE SOUTHERN UÍ NÉILL
0
80Kms
0
50Mls

The Laigin

Flanking Munster on the east was the overlordship of the
Laigin, with the Osraige forming a long buffer state along
the Nore valley, between the Eóganacht of Cashel and the
Laigin proper, who lay mainly to the east of the Barrow.
The Laigin themselves split fairly neatly into those of the
north and those of the south. These are subdivided further:
the northern Laigin into those of Cualu, around the
north-east shoulder of the Wicklow mountains, the Uí
Dúnlainge, controlling the lowland bounded by the
Wicklow mountains on the east, the Liffey on the north
and the territory of the Uí Bairrche to the south; these
latter lay to the north of the Castlecomer plateau and west
of the Barrow. In the territory of the southern Laigin the
Uí Ceinnselaigh predominated, with subordinate to them
the Uí Felmeda in the upper Slaney valley and the Uí
Drona a little to the south-west of these latter. To the north
of the Uí Drona lay the territory of the Fothairt. In the
coastal lowland south from Wicklow head were the Uí
Enechglais, and to the north of these again the Uí Garrchon,
not counted as a branch of the ruling dynasty.

To the north of the Osraige, protecting the flanks of
the northern Laigin against the kingdom of Cashel, and
more or less sandwiched between the Slieve Bloom
mountains and the Castlecomer plateau, lay the Laígis,
and yet further north the more important and substantial
kingdom of Uí Failgi, newly emergent. The Laigin by
this time ruled no further north than a line drawn by the
Liffey and its tributary the Rye; and into the gap between
the boundaries of the Uí Failgi and the northern Laigin
and the Shannon, projected an area ruled by branches of
the Uí Néill.

The Connachta

West of the Shannon, separated from the Dál gCais to
the south by the Slieve Aughty range and flanked on the

36

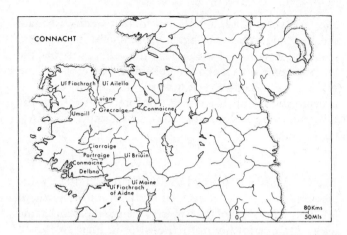

CONNACHT

east by the barrier of Loch Derg, lay the Uí Maine, controlling the greater part of the lowlands stretching north as far as Ahascragh and Ballinasloe; between Slieve Aughty and the sea lay the territory of the Uí Fiachrach of Aidne. To the north of these, in the lowland east of Loch Mask, the smooth rolling land between Shannon and Suck, and the gentle valley between the Clare and the Suck, was Uí Briúin land. Between them, the Uí Maine, Uí Fiachrach and Uí Briúin held most of the good land in each Connacht.

To their west, beyond Loch Corrib and Loch Mask, lay successively the Delbna and Conmaicne, in the boggy lowland and mountain country, mainly in the coastal belt. North, around Loch Mask and in the network of deep valleys in the uplands, were the Partraige and north again the Ciarraige: to the west of these, and to the north of the Conmaicne, on the passably good soils of the lowlands around Clew Bay, lay the Umaill.

The north-west and north, with an abundance of boggy heath and lakes, improving to good arable and pasture as it approached the Moy, was the domain of the northern Uí Fiachrach, with the Uí Ailella in the lowlands west of the Ox mountains and towards the coast; along the upper

37

Moy valley lay the Luighne, and to their south-east again the Grecraige. East yet again from these, in the lake-spattered lowlands of the upper Erne valley, between the Shannon on the west and the uplands on the east, lay land which, while nominally at least the domain of the Cenél Cairpre, was probably already under pressure from the Uí Briúin. In the same area, also, was another branch of the Conmaicne.

The northern Uí Néill

The Cenél Cairpre were of the Uí Néill, and still constituted a territorial link between the southern and the northern Uí Néill. The north of the country, west of the Bann, came under the overlordship of these latter in their two main branches, the Cenél Conaill and the Cenél nEógain. The former held the land west of the Foyle. It is likely that the desolate mountain heartland of Donegal, which was mainly bog-covered moorland, was uninhabited, save in the valleys. The better lands were parcelled out among branches and collaterals of the ruling family: the Cenél mBógaine held the coastlands running west from the mouth of the Erne, of which only the valleys between the

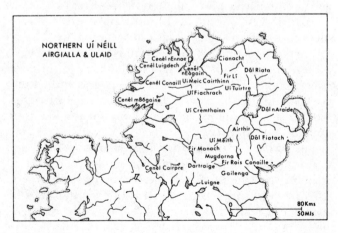

windswept and boggy ridges were of any great use. The lowland fringe of the west, northwest and north, was held by the Cenél Luigdech, while the lowlands of east Donegal, from Mulroy Bay to Loch Swilly and the Foyle, were held by the Cenél nÉnnae. There are traces also of earlier, over-laid, populations, such as, in the Fanad peninsula, the Corbraige, to which Columcille's mother belonged.

The Inishowen peninsula belonged to the Cenél nEógain, and in it lay Aileach, the nominal seat of their kings; whether they had yet begun their expansion south-east is unclear, but probable.

The Airgialla

To the east of the northern Uí Néill, in a line from Loch Foyle to the mouth of the Newry river, lay the Airgialla. Immediately to the south-east of Loch Foyle itself lay the Uí Meic Cairthinn, in the Roe and Faughan valleys, and to the south of these, in the basin of the Foyle and Strule valleys, and on the plateau overlooking the Roe, lay the Uí Fiachrach of Ardstraw, both, like the Uí Tuirtre to the east, claiming descent from Colla Uais.

South again from the Uí Fiachrach, in the Sperrins, were the Uí Cremthainn. To the east of these, bordering the Uí Meic Cairthinn and sandwiched between these and the Fir Lí in the lowland west of the Bann, were the Cianachta of Glenn Gemin, apparently an offshoot of the Cianacht of Brega, and not counted as part of the Airgialla. In the boggy land to their south, and bounded on the south by the northern end of Loch Neagh, lay the Uí Tuirtre. To the south of the Loch, in the drumlin country between the western flanks of the Mournes and the river Blackwater, lay the kingdom of Airthir; to the south-west of this lay the Uí Méith, and to the south-east of these latter, still in the drumlin country, the Mugdorna and the Fir Rois. Behind these, to the west, lay the Fir Manach and the Dartraige, neither of them of the Airgialla.

Ulidia

East of the Bann, in the Main and Bann valleys, and on the Antrim plateau, was the territory of the Dál Riata. South of these lay the lands controlled by the Dál nAraide, extending over the lowlands between Belfast Lough and the Mournes, and eastwards over the low hills bordering Strangford Lough. The Mournes were the preserve of the Dál Fiatach; southwards, in the lowlands beyond Carlingford, lay the plain of Muirtheimne, of uncertain standing, disputed by the Ulaid and the southern Uí Néill: its later inhabitants, the Conaille, were probably already in possession. It filled the gap between Airthir and the sea.

The southern Uí Néill

Southwards as far as the Liffey was the territory of the Uí Néill of the south: ruled by the kings of Uisnech, with subordinate dynasties of the Uí Néill – the Cenél Lóegaire west of Tara, claiming descent from Lóegaire son of Niall; the Cenél nArdgaile to the south of these, claiming descent from Ardgal son of Conall Cremthainne; and an emergent dynasty in Brega, covering most of the south-eastern section of the territory of the southern Uí Néill. West, in the lowlands towards the Shannon, was the kingdom of Tethba, ruled by another Uí Néill dynasty; and in the south, bordering the Uí Failgi, lay the territory of the Cenél Fiachach.

Scattered among the Uí Néill kingdoms were various subordinate peoples: on the coast, straddling the Boyne, lay the Cianachta, and between these and the Airgialla to the north-east were the Gailenga and Luigne, peoples of which other branches were to be found in Connachta, suppliers of fighting men. To the south of Tara itself was the Déisi of Tara, to their west the Fir Thulach, and further south-west, south of Tethba and west of the Cenél Fiachach, bordering the Shannon and the Uí Maine on the far side, the Delbna.

These peoples are detectable with varying degrees of certainty in the late sixth century. Others, offshoots of these, were at the time in process of formation under the surface, to emerge at a later period into the light. What kind of society existed in these kingdoms, and what kind of bonds held it together?

3 Kingship and Society

Status and honour

The society which thus comes into the half-light was heavily stratified: a small layer of kings above a larger layer of nobles, themselves overlaying the mass of commoners who formed the base of the pyramid. Within these layers can be distinguished yet further strata, fairly precisely definable in the case of royalty, less so in the case of the nobles and the commoners.

Status among commoners was assessed primarily on one's possessions, by the extent to which one was economically independent or not. Among the nobles, standing was measured by the size of one's vassalry of clients – the possession of such a vassalry was precisely what distinguished nobles from commoners. Among kings, standing was assessed by the number of *tuath*s subordinate to one, and the level of subordination.

It is difficult to exaggerate the importance of status and honour in early Irish society. Honour (*enech*, literally 'face') is defined in terms of so many units of cattle in a scale rising in proportion to status. Thus, an ordinary *bó-aire*, an independent farmer, had an honour-price of six *sét*s, which a law-text of *c.* 700 estimates as worth almost five milch-cows; the king of a *tuath*, the lowest level of king, had an honour-price of seven *cumal*s, which on the evidence of the same text works out at not less than forty-nine milch-cows. The value attached to the *sét* and the *cumal* varied, of course, from time to time, but the proportions between honour-prices of various social levels remained constant.

One's honour-price defined, at least in the classical period, the limits of what one could legally do. If involved in a lawsuit, one's oath, whether exculpatory or in rebuttal, was worth no more than one's honour-price: a person of higher social status, and hence higher honour-price, could 'overswear' one. The value of evidence on one or the other side was, conveniently, assessed by the honour-price of the witnesses: the higher the honour-price, the greater the value attached to that person's evidence. In the same way, no man might act as surety where an amount greater than his honour-price was involved. These restrictions, to a great extent merely common-sensical in their social context, may indeed not have obtained in the 'archaic' period, that is, the sixth century; but by the seventh century, the 'classical' period, they were accepted as the norm.

Honour could be outraged in well-nigh innumerable ways. Most legal wrongs were considered as outrages to honour, in varying degrees, and involved the offender in payment of a proportion of the injured party's honour-price, in serious cases the whole; and for persons of dependent status, such as wives, and sons still living in their father's household, compensation for offences against them was calculated as a proportion of the honour-price of their 'principal' – to be paid to this latter, not to the injured party himself. Not that such payments exhausted the penalties due: damage to person and property also had to be made good, if nothing else. One's own honour could be forfeited for such grave illegalities as giving false testimony, or defaulting as a surety, with consequent loss of all rights attached to one's status until amends had been made – which also reduced the penalties if an enemy chose that particular time to work off a grudge against one.

This prickly awareness of status naturally had political consequences. 'Face' as a motive and occasion of political, including military, action cannot be underestimated in this period. The death of Cummascach son of Áed had as its ostensible motive his behaviour in claiming the right to sleep with the wife of Bran Dub, king of the Laigin and his host; and the death of his father Áed, king of Tara, in the following year, was occasioned by an attempt to avenge his son – or so it was believed; the battle of Moira was believed to have been ultimately occasioned by a slight inflicted on Congal Cláen, king of the Ulaid. Whether these be factually correct or not, they are socially true in being the type of reaction which was found natural.

At the level of the commoner and of the noble, acknowledging a superior, disputes could in the last resort be referred to this latter; at a higher level, however, compensation was almost impossible to obtain in the same way, and a sense of injury could usually be assuaged only by violence against the injurer. In most cases, there is no need to look for a more subtle motive for bloodshed than a sense of grievance on the one hand, or – in the upper levels of society – the desire to succeed another in a position of power, or to keep the power one already has. In most cases such a position is that of king, but cases are known where it was an abbacy.

The office of kingship

The basic political unit of Irish society was the *tuath*: the basic political person was the king, masculine to the feminity of the *tuath,* to which he was bound, and which was bound to him, in a kind of wedlock. The inauguration of a king was, symbolically, a mating with the local goddess, with the object of bringing fertility to man and beast in his reign. Such symbolic matings are recorded of Tara, of Emain, and of Croghan, and were probably widespread. The rites involved, whatever they were, were of unambiguously pagan character, and lapsed with the general acceptance of Christianity; the *feis* or 'mating' of Tara lapsed in the mid-sixth century, with the general christian-

44

isation of the Uí Néill, and no doubt other such 'matings' disappeared, or had already done so, when their time had come. The fundamental notion of the rites, the concept of the king as spouse of the *tuath*, however, persisted for many centuries, untouched by sporadic attempts to christianise the inauguration of kings.

In some sense, a king in early Ireland, more particularly in pagan Ireland, was a sacred person, kingship a sacred position. In theory, he should be physically unblemished, and while, again theoretically, a king who acquired a blemish was thereby disqualified from the kingship, in the historical period at least kings are known, such as Congal Cáech 'the one-eyed', king of Ulaid, whose sobriquet implies the possession of such a blemish. Very likely only blemishes which affected his fighting ability counted in practice. Equally important, he should be morally unblemished, for on the justice of his rule depended the prosperity of his people – cows giving milk in abundance, good crops of corn, fruit and mast, good fishing, temperate weather; by his rule plagues, famines and other natural visitations were averted, and peace assured within his *tuath*, and victory over enemies without. The rule of an unrighteous king, conversely, drew down on his *tuath* precisely the opposite. Whether in fact any king was ever deposed – and deposition usually meant, in the historical period at least, his death – because of the occurrence of plague or famine, poor corn crops or other such misfortunes, is far from clear; defeat in battle, however, if the king were not killed therein, is a not implausible occasion for deposition, although again no example of this can be quoted.

Since the king was the 'head' of the *tuath*, his death in battle was by definition the defeat of his *tuath*; if he decided that prudence was to be preferred to heroism and broke off the battle, that also was by definition the defeat of his *tuath*. There are indeed traces in later tradition of the appointment of a stand-in, a 'battle-smiter', to conduct battles on the king's behalf and thus avoid the embarrassment of his death or defeat. Conversely, an exploit performed by one of his army was regarded as his: when an entry in the annals notes that *A* king of X killed *B* king of Y, it does not mean that *A* in fact was even within spear-throwing distance of *B* in battle. Thus, when Conall Guthbind is credited with killing Áed Sláine in 604, what it in fact means is that Áed was slain by Áed Guastan, Conall's fosterbrother, and one Báegal Bile, acting on behalf of Conall.

The sacred character of the king is further emphasised by the tabus or *gessa* attached to him. The notion of such tabus is of course far from uncommon in early Irish literature and mythology, but such prohibitions were normally attached to persons, not, as here, to an office. Those attached to the office of king of a particular dynasty may in some cases reflect an action which had in the remote past proved unfortunate for a king of that dynasty; but in others no such explanation seems plausible. For the king of Tara it was tabu, *geis,* to be still in bed at sunrise when in the plain round Tara, to break a journey on Wednesday in the plain of Brega, to strike his horses in *Fán Cummair* (which is unidentified), to enter north Tethba on a Tuesday, to travel over *Magh Cuilinn* – around Cooksborough in Meath – after sunset, and other actions still more opaque; for the king of Connacht, two of the actions which were *geis* to him were to make a circuit of Croghan at *Samhain,* the first of November and one of the turning-points of the pagan year, and to go in a cloak of many colours on a dappled grey horse on the heath of Lowhed, in Clare. The latter may fairly be linked with a tradition of a defeat of the men of Connacht at Lowhed.

Corresponding to these tabus were a series of lucky things for the king. In the case of the king of Tara, these were connected with the feast of Lugnasad, the first of

August, and consisted of the consumption of various foods – fish from the Boyne, venison from *Luibnech,* bilberries from *Brí Léith* (near Ardagh) and so forth. Other, less mystical, lucky things are found in the case of other kings: the king of Cashel was commended to despoil Croghan at the call of the cuckoo, to burn the northern Laigin, and to chant the passion in Lent at Cashel – the only Christian reference in the series; the king of the Ulaid was commended to begin his expedition always from Emain Macha, to spend three nights there with his weapons before crossing his southern frontier, and to take hostages as far north as Dunseverick in Antrim. This more severely practical, not to say military, note is more perceptible in the lists of fortunate things than in the tabus.

This sacral character is by the historical period in process of contraction. There is no trace of its having extended to the exercise of any priestly or vatic functions, which in the pre-Christian period were exercised by the druids. Nor does it extend to functioning as judge, at least in the historic period; mythical kings such as Cormac son of Art are credited with having been judges and law-makers, but in the historic period this is the function of a specialised class of jurisconsults, whose business was to preserve, transmit (in verse) and apply the law, which was deemed immutable, in disputes between members of different kin-groups. The king's only law-making function is that of issuing ordinances of a temporary nature in an emergency, for such matters as saving a threatened harvest or for repelling an invasion.

The process of contraction can be illustrated by the case of a man with a grievance against the king. In principle, a king was exempt from suit: an early legal maxim sums it up as 'A king's honour (literally "face") is too great to be claimed against.' Originally the only method of compelling a king to come to arbitration was the remarkable archaic procedure of fasting against him. By the historic period, this is a highly conventionalised ritual, probably evolved from a fast, if necessary, to the death, which is employed only against those who were *nemed* 'holy', such as king, bishop or poet; but there is evidence that at the dawn of the historic period the term was applied more widely, to almost every kind of craftsman. The person harbouring a grievance, after notifying his claim, carried out a fast overnight (the period including the main meal of the day) in some place where he could be seen, such as before the *nemed's* door. The person thus 'fasted against' might himself not eat, and by the following morning at latest he was expected to give the fasting person a pledge or offer some satisfactory surety that the matter would be submitted to arbitration. To disregard the fasting person entailed complete loss of face.

This procedure, then, represents a formalisation and limitation of the primitive procedure. In the historic period, a second method became available to a plaintiff against the king: he might sue, in the normal way, a commoner, the *aithech fortha* 'substitute commoner', who had been specifically designated to answer private claims against the king, thereby eliminating any risk of loss of face. By the ninth century, indeed, this procedure had been further extended: a plaintiff might, in the absence of a 'substitute commoner', sue in the usual way any commoner of the king's household.

The royal face might be lost in other ways. To be found using a maul or axe or spade – the tools of a commoner – was below the king's dignity. Nor should a king go round unaccompanied: the retinue prescribed for the king of a *tuath* when on private business was nine, on public business twelve – although, this being a rural and agricultural society, in the month of sowing he might be accompanied by only his judge and two others.

Dignity and 'face' could co-exist with Christianity where the more explicitly pagan characteristics of kingship could not. These latter faded out, leaving however an enduring residue of their presuppositions. The fertility ceremony associated with the inauguration of a king, as pointed out above, lapsed during the sixth century. A Christian colouring was given to the early 'mirror for princes' called the *Testament of Morann* – a mythical juris-consult. Such an expression of the primitive as the *óenach* persisted: an assembly of the *tuath* held at regular intervals, at which, in addition to such diversions as horse-racing and athletic contests, important public business such as the notification of the conclusion of a treaty with a neighbour, or the proclamation of outlaws, might be dealt with. In addition to its practical functions, and its value as entertain-ment, the *óenach* was another means of ensuring good fortune. Thus the *óenach* of Carman, the *óenach* of the Laigin, held somewhere along the River Barrow, if held as prescribed every third year, from the first of August (the feast of Lugnasad) to the eighth, reputedly ensured for the Laigin corn and milk, mast and fish, and freedom from aggression by any outsider. Such deep-rooted traditions could not be jettisoned, and had perforce to be tolerated and as far as possible christianised. Thus in 784 the *óenach* of Teltown (*Tailtiu*) was sanctified by the relics of Erc of Slane.

The kin-group and society

Just as the *tuath* was the basic political unit, so within the *tuath* the basic social unit was the family, but the family defined in a very precise way and perhaps best referred to by the Irish term, *fine,* which we translate 'kin-group'. It included much more than the conjugal family of parents and children: it was, rather, a group made up, primarily, of all those males who had a great-grandfather in common, that is, up to and including second cousins. This is some-times called the *derbfine,* the 'certain kin', in implied contrast to a possible wider kin-group which in certain

Fig. 5.

THE EARLY IRISH KINSHIP GROUP

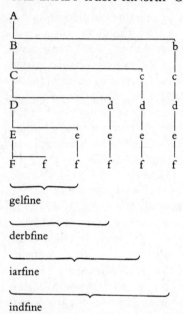

infrequent circumstances might have a function: the *iarfine*, a five-generation group, and the *indfine*, a six-generation group, neither of which came into play unless the *derbfine* became extinct, in which case the latter's patrimony passed to the *iarfine*, or failing this again, to the *indfine*. Outside this six-generation group, the rights and responsibilities of kinship lapsed.

Within the *derbfine*, in the classical period, is visible the emergence of a smaller kinship group, the *gelfine*, the descendants of a common grandfather, that is, a three-generation group which, while not superseding the *derbfine* in its functions, yet fulfils all the practical requirements of the kin-group.

On the *fine* pivoted the greater part of one's claims, obligations and loyalties. Each man in the *fine* might be liable, in varying degrees, for the consequences of another member's actions: if one of them slew a member of another *fine* and was unable to pay the fixed wergild of seven *cumals*, plus the full 'honour-price' appropriate to the rank of the slain, his *fine* was liable for it. For the same reason, a member of the *fine* could not accept a 'free' fief from a lord without the consent of the *fine*, since it was ultimately liable for any default of render on his part – and the render of a 'free' fief was notably heavy; entering base clientship, however, did not require the consent of the *fine*. By the same token, all contracts and engagements entered into by the head of the *fine* – usually the eldest member – required the consent of all members in good standing. This primary loyalty to the *fine* dictated that, wherever possible, buying and selling, contracts and clientship, should be arranged with fellow members of the *fine*; in some respects, indeed, the *fine* often acted as a kind of cooperative for such matters as joint ploughing, where individual members did not possess a full plough-team of oxen. If a member died childless, he could not bequeath his inherited land to anyone he chose: it passed to other male members of the *fine* in proportions varying with the closeness of their blood kinship to the deceased. The alienation of any part of one's inherited land required ratification by all full members of the *fine*, which would not be readily forthcoming; only land not acquired by inheritance could be disposed of more or less at will, and if it passed by inheritance to one's sons, ceased thereby to be readily alienable.

Each generation gave rise, naturally, to a fresh *fine*, so that where there were male descendants there was a perpetual hiving-off process. Women did not count: if they married, they passed to their husband's *fine* for the length of the marriage (some marriages were merely temporary arrangements); if left unmarried, they remained subject to their father, or after his death, their elder brother (for whom there is a special term, *amnair*), or their nearest and eldest male kinsman; if widowed, they were subject to their sons, if these were of full age, or otherwise to their father or elder brother. The original total incapacity of women in legal matters – for example, their inability to enter contracts without the consent of their principal, be he husband, father, brother or son – is in the classical period beginning to be eroded by the occurrence of female heirs to lands to which there was no male heir – perhaps in part a by-product of the havoc wrought by the plague epidemics of 664–5 and 683. Even in this latter case, the lands were not alienable at will, but passed on the death of the female heir, if she herself had no male heir, to the nearest male member of the *fine*.

The conjugal family does indeed receive some recognition within this kin-group. Father and son, mother and daughter, are acknowledged to be linked by a special bond even closer than that of ordinary blood-kinship; but it is designated by a term (*lánamnas*) which is used also of the bond between foster-parent and foster-child, between a teacher and his pupil, between an abbot and his monk. All these in a sense, the same basic sense, are a unit. The father may, if he chooses, veto any and every contract his son enters into, while his son is still living in his household; the same is true of the other 'pairs'. But the other member of the pair has, correspondingly, some slight right in the matter: the subject son can veto any disadvantageous contracts his father enters into.

Loyalty to one's kin being the primary obligation, how was it possible to exact performance of an obligation from the outsider? Much depended on the nature of the obligation. Obligations of mutual advantage presented no serious problem; but obligations arising out of delicts, such as damage caused by another's trespassing cattle, were a more thorny matter. Ideally, the owner of the offending cattle could make good the amount of damage without demur; but in practice there might be counterbalancing circumstances, such as the other's ill-kept fence, which might mitigate one's negligence: the makings of a long-drawn-out wrangle.

The main resource available in such a case was distraint, the impounding of the other's chattels more or less as hostages to compel him to submit to arbitration. The distinctions drawn by the early jurists are numerous and substantial, but in its essentials the procedure was straightforward. The first stage was the notification of claim, followed by a delay to allow the other party to consider his position; then a formal seizure, though not removal, of chattels, which still remained in the debtor's hands. The formal seizure might be ticklish, and it was advisable to be accompanied by a man of law. Thereafter followed another delay, after which one proceeded to the formal removal of chattels to a pound, with a formal notification to the debtor of the place of impounding. Finally, after a further delay, the chattels impounded became the property of the distrainor, if the alleged debtor showed no inclination to submit the matter to law.

This procedure has of course its parallel on the larger, political, scale: many of the raids recorded in the annals were probably, in substance, seizure of chattels from a subordinate and recalcitrant *tuath,* naturally without the formality attendant on distraint, though it is to be presumed that some kind of notification of claim had been made beforehand. Most conflicts between *tuaths,* whether between those on the same level or those in a relationship of subordination, involved no loss of territory. The normal procedure was to cross the border of the offending *tuath* with a hosting, seize as many head of cattle and horses, and any other valuables lying around, as possible, and return home. If the other *tuath* were able to gather in time sufficient men to resist, there might then be a battle. None of these were very elaborate affairs, from a military point of view; arms were limited to spear, shield, and sword (not always of very good metal); the first stage could be the casting of light throwing-spears, after which, in the mêlée, either the bigger spears called *craísech* which could be wielded halberd-fashion, or if there were no room for this, the sword could be used. This might be preceded by individual challenges to combat, well larded with insults, in the fashion surviving from the ages of chaos; and if the kings on both sides could be fired to engage in this fashion, the matter might be settled with considerable economy of life, since the king's defeat was the defeat of his *tuath*. Failing a battle, the other *tuath* would carry out a similar raid as soon as it was in a position to do so. These were the small change of politics.

The kin-group and kingship

The kingship of any given *tuath* was the possession of the ruling kindred: it was the royal lineage that counted, not the claims of any individual within that lineage. No member thereof could lay claim to succeed automatically to the kingship, by primogeniture or otherwise; in theory, all those descended from a previous king down to a remove of four generations were eligible for the kingship, and, given the high fertility of some kings, a very large circle of such eligibles often existed. If, for example, we take the nine generations of rulers of the Cenél nEógain from their founder Eógan down to Niall Frossach, we find that they are credited with an average of four sons each – Eógan is credited with ten, which brings up the average slightly; if each of these somewhat theoretical sons kept up the average, by the fourth generation there would be 256 males all with an equal theoretical claim to the kingship. Of the four sons of Fergal son of Máel Dúin, one, Conchobor, is credited with overfulfilling his norm with twelve sons.

In reality, of course, many were ruled out at an early stage. Some might well have been begotten of slave-girls, whose offspring had no claim to succeed to lordship – nor probably, the sons of any woman of semi-servile condition. Others would have perished, naturally or by violence, before a chance of kingship occurred; many others would of necessity have been eliminated on grounds of extreme age or youth, yet others by physical disqualification, if unable to fight, or temperamental, if lacking ambition. More would be counted out by inability to gather a following within the kindred to support any claim they might make. Yet when all these had been discounted, there could still remain a substantial nucleus of claimants to kingship qualifying on all counts.

In the case of property, the inheritance of which followed the same rules, no great problem arose: land was divided equally between sons, or where sons were lacking passed to brothers, nephews and other kin in a predetermined sequence. As with property, most successions passed to brothers or sons, fewer to grandsons or nephews, fewer still to more remote kin. But kingship was not essentially divisible. It is true that cases did occur where two contending factions within a kindred were so evenly matched that neither was able to impose its candidate on the other; this happened among the Ulaid in the ninth century, and for a time there might be a joint kingship, with, in effect, two kings. Such arrangements were essentially impermanent. Kingdoms might split, as with the kingdom of Brega at the beginning of the eighth century; fresh kingdoms might emerge from a greater kingship, as the royal line of Brega from the southern Uí Néill at the beginning of the seventh century, or the Uí Briúin kingships of Umall and Bréifne, which emerge as entities in their own right in the middle of the eighth century. But as a general rule, one *tuath*, one king.

The commonest device to avoid a bloody struggle on a

king's death was to nominate beforehand, with the agreement, willing or unwilling, of those eligible, and the assent, perhaps tacit, of the notables of the *tuath*, a successor designate (*tánaise*). Such an institution is recognised in a law-tract of *c.* 700, and there are earlier examples of it, most notably in Dál Riata, where Eochu Buide, Áedán son of Gabrán's successor and his son, was nominated in his father's lifetime – naturally, by his father. It did not, of course, always work out in practice. A king of the oppressive type called the 'bull-lord' (*tarbflaith*) might designate a particular son as successor, but as the early text which portrays him points out, the impotent resentment felt for him during his lifetime would very likely be transferred, no longer impotent, after his death to his sons, who would not inherit.

Survival as king: hostages, marriage and fosterage

Even when accepted by the *tuath* and his kindred, the new king usually found it prudent to insure against the aristocratic kindreds' swinging away from him later to support a rival; and the normal means of doing so was by taking from them hostages whose life would be forfeited by their kin's defection. So normal was this that to release one's hostages was regarded as equivalent to abdication.

Apart from this type of insurance, alliance by marriage presented one possible means of consolidating one's position against external and internal enemies; not in fact a particularly strong means. Marriage to a man's daughter or sister implied no more than that, at the time, he was willing to hand over the lady in question with her dowry and accept the bride-price in return. It did not bind him automatically or even habitually to support his in-law in disputes, and indeed there are examples of husbands and fathers-in-law who were at some point in their careers bitter enemies: Bécc of Bairrche was married to Conchend, daughter of Congal Cennfota, king of Ulaid, but this seems to have in no way inhibited him from killing Congal in 674. At best, by taking or giving a daughter in marriage, one acquired a potential ally. Ethne Uathach, daughter of Crimthann son of Énnae Cennselach, was believed to have married Óengus son of Nad Fraích, king of Cashel, and to have drawn him on the side of the Uí Ceinnselaig into the battle of *Cenn Losnada* about 490, in which they lost to the northern Laigin represented by Illand son of Dúnlang, abetted by Muirchertach Mac Erca, of the Uí Néill. This may not in fact be true; but it illustrates what early Irish society believed to be plausible.

There were indeed some cases where support by one's in-laws could be almost automatic. By marriage, a woman passed from her paternal kin-group to that of her husband. Some slight links with her own kin remained, the more substantial, the less formal the marriage was: a chief wife of the same social standing as her husband was the most loosely linked to her kin. These latters' rights were limited to intervention if her husband neglected his duty of providing appropriate education to the children of the marriage, and to a payment of one-seventh of the wergild if any of the children were killed – this in addition to the wergild payable to the deceased's paternal kin. In cases of this kind, the maternal kin might as a rule be counted to support action taken either to levy the wergild, or to exact vengeance – if only as a matter of face. On these grounds, then, it is always worth while to note the maternal kin of the men of violence who dominated Irish society, when possible; it may provide another bone for the skeleton, usually sadly incomplete, of political interactions.

Of at least equal importance with the none too certain political advantages of marriage was the necessity of marrying a woman of equal rank – a fundamental question of 'face'. The record of the marriages of some kings of the Laigin in the seventh-eighth century seems to show both considerations in operation: Murchad (†727) allied himself to another branch of the Laigin by marrying a daughter of Cellach of Cualu, Conchend; Cellach of Cualu (†716) himself had allied himself to the minor Laigin lineage of Uí Bairrche; but Murchad's father, Bran (†695), had taken a wife from the Dál Riata, who could be of no possible military assistance to him.

Finally, the most important function of marriage in Irish society was to supply sons. Mac Cáirthind, reputed ancestor of the Uí Meic Cáirthind in Airgialla, was said to have had twelve sons, of whom four were by slave girls; Fland Dá Chongal, king of Uí Failge, is credited with the same number, with the same proportion by a slave girl. Such fertility was expected at that level, and admired; but with a heavy infant mortality, it was rarely attainable without a plurality of wives. Offspring begotten of slave girls had the further advantage that, having no claim to succeed to their father's kingship, they were totally dependent on him, or on the half-brother who perhaps succeeded him, for any advancement – a substantial motive for loyalty. The church disapproved, predictably, of such pluralities of wives: the Irish collection of canons compiled early in the eighth century includes the canon of an earlier, Irish, synod, which exhorts kings – not perhaps as one convinced of prevailing – that 'the greater the dignity a king has received, the greater should be the fear he has; for many women debase his soul, and his spirit, divided by a multitude of spouses, slips deeply into sin.' Unfortunately, the examples of the Old Testament patriarchs enabled the native jurists to point out, demurely, that 'God's chosen people lived in plurality of unions, so that it is not easier to condemn it than to praise it.' However much one's sons might quarrel between themselves, they would at any rate be expected to support one against a less close, and ambitious, kinsman with an eye on the kingship.

More binding than the ties of marriage were those

created by fosterage, the placing of a child under the care of a foster-father and mother from the age of seven to seventeen (for boys) or fourteen (for girls). This might be done gratuitously, by a kinsman, or for a fee, which might be land; it might even be combined with giving the child as a hostage to one's king or over-king. The foster-parents undertook to provide for and educate the child in a manner befitting his future status. On the child's side this created an obligation at least as strong as those of filial piety; the foster-parents were known by terms, *aite* and *muime,* which in origin were child language ('daddy' and 'mammy'); the slaying of a foster-parent was parricide (or matricide), sexual commerce with them incest. Just as a plurality of wives was, for obvious economic reasons, a prerogative of the rich, so too a plurality of foster-parents was a mark of high social standing – though naturally only one pair were saddled with rearing the child in question; and by this means the child, come to manhood, might find himself, if politically ambitious, supplied with a number of ready-made allies; and indeed, since common fosterage created a bond also, those who had shared his fosterage might also be counted as allies.

Economy and society: clientship

At the basic level of the *tuath,* the successful bidder for kingship could expect to live in only moderately greater comfort than before, with the slighter greater pomp appropriate to his new state. His pastimes, as before, would be drinking, feasting, the chase and, if so inclined, warfare. He would not have been much richer than the more prosperous of his subjects and kin: a jurist of *c.* 700, with a passion for systematising, laid down that the house of the king of a *tuath* should be thirty-seven feet long, while that of the highest of the aristocracy should be thirty feet. To this comparative simplicity of dwelling corresponded an equal simplicity of administration: a *rechtaire* 'steward' to ensure that the king's orders were carried out, a juris-consult to arbitrate on matters to which the king was a party. All others were there *pro magnifico*: pipers and harpers and jugglers, serving-men of no standing, spear-men to stop brawling at ale.

His revenues differed hardly at all from those of any member of the aristocratic kindreds: the extras attached to kingship were tribute from the free kindreds of the *tuath,* and the enjoyment of mensal land which passed at death, not to the heirs of his body (as would his own land), but to his successor. For the rest, like any other aristocrat, he was entitled to labour service and renders of cattle, milk and milk products, corn, malt and meat from his own clients.

Clientship was the basic economic underpinning of the upper classes, aristocracy or kings, and a basic social necessity for the lower classes, whom it provided with a certain measure of protection against arbitrary violence – at least by persons other than their lords. It therefore requires a moderately detailed exposition.

Clientship was of two kinds, free and base, and consisted essentially in the handing over to a client (*céle*) by a lord of a fief or 'favour' (*rath*), in return for which the client was bound to make certain precisely defined renders to the lord.

The nature and conditions of the renders, however, differed sharply in the two kinds of clientship. In free clientship, the client was bound to render one third the amount of the fief each year in the first three years of clientship: thus, if the free client had received three cows in fief, the lord by the end of the third year would have received a total render of three cows, that is, the full amount of the fief given. If the relationship were maintained for a further three years, the yearly render was then paid in the produce of the cattle in milk and calves, again up to one third the value of the cattle; and if the relationship were maintained for yet a seventh year, this was free of render.

These are the principal renders; but they were accompanied by subordinate renders in kind in flitches of bacon, sacks of malt and wheat, and supplies of pork and butter.

All in all, these were burdensome terms; but the burden was counterbalanced by the possibility for either lord or client of ending the relationship at any time by, in effect, returning whatever each had to the other's credit: the client by returning the fief itself, the lord by returning, in kind, any renders standing to the client's credit.

The immaterial renders on both sides are simply summarised: by accepting a man as his client, the lord undertook to defend his client's rights; the client in turn bound himself to personal (including military) service to his lord, and to pay him due respect by rising in his presence.

Such obligations are common to both kinds of clientship, free and base; but base clientship, while in some material respects less burdensome than free clientship, entailed for the client other obligations.

In the first place, base clientship, unlike free clientship, could not be terminated whenever the client wished. It might, naturally, be ended by mutual consent; if both client and lord had fulfilled their obligations, each could return what the other had given him, and due allowance made for renders paid in advance – although no allowance was due to the lord for any deterioration in the fief brought about by age or use. In all other cases, however, the lord had the whip hand. He might, if he so chose, end the clientship whether the client wished it or not, provided he renounced one third of the value of the fief – assuming that he was not accusing the client of failure in his render or the respect due him. If, however, the client wished to part company with his lord, not moved by disrespect nor by any failure in his obligations on the lord's part, nor to go to another lord, but merely to be his own man, he would have to return twice the amount of the fief; if renders were in arrears, these also were doubled, not counting the fine to which the lord was entitled for the arrears; and even if the renders were not in arrears, those of the year in which the clientship was terminated were doubled.

If the clientship were terminated because the lord had failed in his obligations, this was accomplished merely by each returning what he had received; but if on account of the base client's failure, this failure was assimilated to theft and the client treated as if he had stolen the fief, so that he would be bound to return not only twice the amount of the fief and of any arrears of render – one of the most likely forms of failure on a client's part – but also to pay a fine and an amount calculated on the honour-price of his lord. If again the client were to try to end the relationship from 'insolence', he was bound to a double return plus the honour-price of his lord, and if no 'insolence' were involved, but merely a wish to transfer to another lord, he would still have to pay twice the fief and renders, and half the lord's honour-price. On this there was a limitation: if the second lord to whom the client wished to transfer were of higher standing than the first – and hence better able to protect a client in his rights – the lord abandoned was entitled only to half his honour-price and twice the fief, plus any arrears of render – these however not doubled; and if the second lord had the yet stronger claim of kinship with the client, the proportion of the first lord's honour-price payable was reduced to one third.

Payment of honour-price was incurred by the slur on the lord implicit in quitting him for another; conversely, if the lord demanded his fief back as a means of insulting his client, the latter was entitled to deduct the amount of his honour-price from the fief before returning two thirds of it. If the general rule that no man might accept a fief of greater value than his honour-price were strictly kept, this amounted to forfeiture to the client; but in fact one might take as much in fief as one could handle. If it were demanded to give as a fief to another client, with no insult involved, the client was entitled to deduct from it half his honour-price, unless, again, the other client were of higher rank, or closer in blood to the lord, or if his render was more necessary to the lord than that of the first client; in that case the amount deductible fell to one third of the client's honour-price.

In all these cases, obviously, the lord holds the trump cards. For minor failures on the client's part, the lord could in any case act as judge and jury in his own case and fine the client if he wished; but quite apart from this, the enormous penalties which might be exacted from a base client who proposed to sever the relationship would as a rule be more than sufficient to inhibit any attempt to do so. It is quite conceivable that an attempt to do so would involve the client in penalties which he would be unable to pay, penalties which might then be treated by the lord as further fiefs, for which renders would be due, so enmeshing the client in a continuing subordination to the lord. It is not suggested that this was common – we have no evidence either way – but the possibility was obviously there. Where failure on the lord's part was claimed by the client, the difficulties of enforcing such a claim, or proving it, were very substantial; for the lord's oath would outweigh that of the client every time. In short, base clientship was a relationship from which the client could buy himself out, but only at a grossly inflated price.

The benefits of base clientship

The advantages of the relationship to the client were both economic and social. Economic, because the direct renders for a fief in base clientship were substantially lower than those of a free fief – less than a sixth of the latter – and the amount of the fief correspondingly higher: for the ordinary *bó-aire*, the self-sufficient commoner, a fief of 30 *séts* – roughly 24 milch-cows – is quoted with a render of one milch-cow yearly and a number of accessory renders. It was in effect a crude system of leasing: not only cattle could be given in fief, but also land, goats, sheep, oxen – the 'tractor of the Iron Age' – hens and iron implements such as bill-hooks and axes; and for each a proportionate and appropriate render was worked out. For a bill-hook, for example, a suggested render was four bundles of faggots in the first year and two every successive year.

For the base client there was also a further material advantage, in that the lord made him a payment equal in value to the client's honour-price, which entitled the lord to a share in compensation paid to the client for injuries inflicted on him, such as bodily harm and theft. To this corresponded the social advantage that the lord was thereby further committed to protecting him, for the profit to be derived from his share of compensation.

Correspondingly, the lord gained certain material advantages from the clientship. He gained an almost guaranteed food-supply, since in return for the fief of 30 *séts* to a *bó-aire*, for example, he was entitled to a render of one cow a year, with its subordinate renders – which were substantial. These latter are enumerated as lard and suet, two calves for consumption in summer, a wether, milk, cream and butter, eight sacks or measures of malt, a sack of kiln-dried wheat, twenty-four loaves of specified dimensions, a pig and a calf for consumption in winter, a flitch of salted pork, three handfuls of candles and four handfuls of herbs. Over and above this the lord was entitled to a night's entertainment in the house of each of his base clients between New Year's Day and Shrovetide, at which he might be accompanied by no less than four guests for each such base client he possesses. Such guestings were also claimed by the abbots of certain monasteries from their base clients, but rather more frequently, at Christmas, Easter and Pentecost; the frequency however is counterbalanced by the restriction of their guests to four.

Over and above these renders, the lord was entitled to

personal service from his clients. This covered not only military and escort service, but also labour in building, sowing and harvesting. The 'rule of Patrick' prescribes that monastic base clients should supply a full day's ploughing and the land and seed for it each year; others, minor clients of secular lords, were bound to supply half a day's labour in harvesting at three days' notice.

By possessing clients the lord also gained status, since this was gauged by the number of his vassalry of clients – no clients, no lord; the lowest level of noble was expected to have a vassalry of ten clients, five free, five base. The symmetry and precision so beloved of the early jurists cannot, of course, have been common in reality, but on the other hand they were probably right in implying that the majority of his base clients would have been farmers in quite a small way, obliged to club together to make up a plough-team; the economically self-sufficient farmer would be in a minority.

By present-day standards this latter, the *bó-aire*, would have been quite a substantial farmer. A holding of 21 *cumal*s of land, all due allowance being made for varying qualities of land and poor yields – perhaps a bushel of corn per acre – from the arable, is, at about 700 acres, well worth having; his stated livestock – twenty cows, two bulls, six oxen, twenty pigs, twenty sheep, four boars and two sows – even when considered as no more than a blueprint, is attractive enough; sixteen measures of corn sown, even at the current yield of three for one, was not to be despised. By the classical period, however, when opportunities for bringing new land under cultivation or pasture were becoming comparatively infrequent, to suppose that many such men would be found in base clientship was probably not realistic; the jurists indeed, in one of their infrequent concessions to the tyranny of fact, acknowledged a status less than that of a *bó-aire* and baptised it *óc-aire* 'young *aire*', that is, of recent emergence. This latter, while not economically self-sufficient either in stock or land, yet ranked as a 'person' in Irish law – other, yet lower ranks were either minors or sons still living in their father's household. There may indeed be an echo of this development in the otherwise late life of Gerald of Mayo, which, shorn of its theological trimming, suggests that the great plague of 664-5 was the outcome of famine (for which read malnutrition), itself caused by overpopulation: for 'to each husbandman as his lawful share were assigned nine or seven *iugera* of level land, eight of rough and nine of wood.' While the precise extent of a *iuger* is unknown, the sense clearly is that this amount was insufficient, and the sequence of events is plausible enough.

Changes of status

That there was at least the possibility of moving upwards from the class of commoners into the ranks of the nobility is undoubted: adroit use of the fiefs available in clientship, combined with good husbandry and a fortunate avoidance of murrain – such as the great cattle-plagues of 699-700 and 778-9 – might bring the commoner to that fortunate position where he had a surplus of cattle which could be given out in fief to others less fortunate. This was in some degree the more possible in that a secondary and even a tertiary clientship to other lords was possible and permissible, with fiefs and renders of lesser size than those of the first, and primary, clientship. The giving of fiefs to others did not, however, automatically promote one to the noble class; it might, however, promote one's grandson, if prosperity and the giving of fiefs had been maintained over the next two generations. The first generation of such commoners thriving to lordship was known as a *flaith aithig* 'a commoner lord', whose render from his clients took the form of butter and unslaughtered beasts and corn, to whose malting he had to attend himself; the second generation, while entitled to better renders, had to consume them, in the form of cooked meats and ale, in the house of the client; and only the third generation became a lord, a member of the nobility in the full sense of the term, and entitled to the full services of his clients.

Such cases were probably not common. Most social mobility was of necessity downwards; for under the customary law of inheritance, the land of a *bó-aire* was divided equally between his sons and might well leave none of them with sufficient land to maintain an independent economic status, hence dropping them a step or more in the social scale. For the lord with surplus land, there was therefore a market among land-holders at this level, that of the *óc-aire*, and one early law-text assumes that land is what is normally given in fief to such persons – though stock, presumably, would also be expected. That this might be counterbalanced elsewhere by families in which there were no male heirs, and into which a landless man might marry, is admitted; and among the poorer classes it is possible that sons married later or not at all. Nonetheless, we may take a gradual progression down the social scale, both within the ranks of the commoners, and from the nobility to the commoners, as more frequent than the reverse.

The servile classes

Small farmers such as these formed a labour pool on which the more prosperous farmers and the nobility could draw, within defined limits. They were, however, further supplemented by lower strata of society, such as the *bothach* and the *fuidir*, both of them tenants-at-will who received land, and presumably livestock, in return for uncertain services. The difference between them is unclear, but may have been in the services demanded of them. In a sense they were freer than the base client, since they could part with their lord at any time by giving due notice that they proposed to abandon their holding, and surrendering two-thirds of the product of their husbandry. The *bothach* 'crofter' may have been one whose patrimony by division on inheritance had shrunk to the point where he could not maintain even the status of an *óc-aire*; the *fuidir*, however, is regarded by the early law-texts as being typically gallows-fodder, a wanderer without kin or a fugitive from justice, and likely enough to wander again. If either remained settled on the lord's land for long enough, and their descendants after them, they could decline to the level of the *sen-chléithe*, a serf who was bound to the land and passed with it, when alienated, as an appurtenance. So of Cummén wife of Brethán in the early eighth century, of whom it is said that half of Óchtar Achid belongs to her 'in house and in man' – the men in question being doubtless *sen-chléithe*s; and there is reference elsewhere to fifteen *sen-chléithe*s being given (with their land) as a fosterage-fee.

Lower yet was the slave, male or female, a chattel whose owner possessed the power of life and death over him or her; yet not quite such a chattel that he could be given in fief like cattle. With him ranked the prisoner taken in war who had not been ransomed, who was as much at his captor's mercy as the slave.

The nobility

Overlying this lower stratum, and supported by it, was the class of nobles, identifiable primarily by the possession of a clientage, but dependent ultimately for survival on the possession of sufficient wealth in cattle to advance in fief to clients. As far as lineage is concerned, the nobility in any given *tuath* divides into members of the ruling family and nobles of other kin-groups. Here too a certain amount of downward social mobility is to be expected, perhaps even more than among the commoners, since families of male heirs are liable to be larger. Polygyny was a privilege of wealth – of kings in particular, but also of the nobility. Since no distinction was drawn for purposes of inheritance between sons of a chief wife and those of a secondary wife – when this latter had not been taken to provide the sons a chief wife had failed to provide – a plethora of sons to be provided for could bite deep into the patrimony, with some of the family ending up among the ranks of the commoners.

Nobility was restricted to those whose family had been noble for three generations; but in the vague area between commoners and nobility proper were to be found a number of commoners who for different reasons had risen to some extent out of the ranks of the commoners. Such was the prosperous commoner taking his first steps towards nobility by advancing fiefs to other commoners. Such too was the *aire coisring*, who was himself a commoner, but as head of his kin represented them, and acted as surety *ex officio* for them, in their dealings with such outside authorities as king and church, and in consequence ranked just below the lowest level of the nobility and just above the highest level of commoners; the *aire échta*, who seems to have been a commoner of the *bó-aire* level who ranked with the lowest level of noble in return for performing a public function in the *tuath*, a function which is obscure, but which seems to have consisted of protecting members of another *tuath* pursuing a blood-feud against a member of his own *tuath*.

4　From plague to plague (549–666)

The Uí Néill to 575

The death of Tuathal Máelgarb in 544 left open the way for
Diarmait son of Fergus Cerrbél to seize the kingship of
Tara: open, but far from clear. That he had a struggle to
establish himself therein is clear from the fact that he
was unable to hold the 'feast' or 'mating' of Tara until 558.
On his south the Laigin were indisposed to leave him in
peace, and the obscure years before 558 may well have been
a period of alternating possession of Tara and dispossession,
although no substantial clashes are recorded. To the north,
the Ulaid were hostile; and to the north-west, the northern
Uí Néill were at best uncooperative. Among these latter
the leading figures were Forgus and Domnall, two sons of
Muirchertach Mac Erca, who themselves had, predictably,
an eye on the kingship of Tara. By defeating Ailill Inbanda,
king of Connacht, in the battle of *Cúil Conaire* in 550, they
had substantially cleared the way for a later ally, Áed son
of Eochu Tirmcharna, to gain the kingship of Connacht.
Diarmait's wives, both the mother of Colmán Már and the
mother of Colmán Bec, if the record be accurate, were of
the Conmaicne, who could hardly be expected, even if
willing, to contribute any substantial military aid to bolster
up his position.

These threats to Diarmait's position became concrete
very shortly after he had held the 'feast' of Tara, and
possibly as a consequence thereof. As far as the Ulaid were
concerned, their attitude to him had been made clear by the

Fig. 6.

THE OPPOSING SIDES AT THE BATTLE OF *CÚIL DREIMNE*

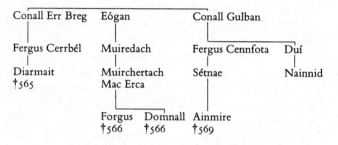

slaying of his son, Colmán Már, by one Dubsloit of the Dál nAraide in the same year as the 'feast'. In 560 he decided to come to grips with the northern Uí Néill, who constituted the most substantial threat at the time, and thrust north-west. At *Cúil Dreimne* in Sligo he was blocked by a combination of the descendants of Eógan and of Conall Gulban, those of Eógan being under the leadership of Forgus and Domnall, and those of Conall under Ainmire son of Sétnae and Nainnid son of Duí; and these were backed up by the king of Connacht, Áed son of Eochu Tirmcharna. Diarmait was soundly defeated; but the northern Uí Néill seem to have been for the moment contented with what was essentially a defensive action, not following it up with any counterthrust. Diarmait's hold on the kingship of Tara itself seems to have remained unshaken, although the effect on his nominal subordinates may well have been unsettling: a year later, at *Cúil Uinsen* in Tethba – itself an Uí Néill kingdom – he was defeated by its king, Áed son of Brénaind. The location of the battle strongly suggests that it was the outcome of a move by Diarmait to re-assert his supremacy over Tethba.

These disasters, nonetheless, he survived by another four years, and in the end perished by the hands of Áed Dub son

71

of Suibne of the Dál nAraide in 565. Here again, the place of his death, Rathbeg in Antrim, implies that the aggressor in this case was Diarmait.

His death was followed by a period of confusion among the Uí Néill. Forgus and Domnall, victors of the battle of *Cúil Dreimne*, were obviously the strongest candidates for the kingship of Tara, and are counted as such by later sources; but in what sense they were kings of Tara, presumably jointly, if in fact they were, is far from clear. They did at least proceed without delay to the first essential for successful rule of Tara, by, as it were, showing the flag to the Laigin, whom they encountered and defeated at their border on the Liffey in 566. Unfortunately for Cenél nEógain prospects, both died in that same year, leaving the succession open to the strongest. Ainmire son of Sétnae, their ally at *Cúil Dreimne* and leader of Conall's descendants, emerged briefly from the ruck, and held the supremacy for three years; in 569 he was slain by a descendant of Eógan, Fergus son of Néillíne, who himself lasted less than a year before being slain in his turn by Áed son of Ainmire.

At this particular time Áed had either no ambitions for supremacy – an intrinsically unlikely supposition – or insufficient support to make worth while a bid for the kingship; for we find dominant for a brief period two descendants of Eógan, one Báetán son of Muirchertach Mac Erca, who must have been fairly advanced in years, and Eochaid, son of the Domnall who died in 566. Apart from this brief supremacy, both are nonentities, and both were slain in 572 by Crónán son of Tigernach, king of Cianachta. The occasion of their death is unclear.

For all practical purposes thereafter the supremacy among the Uí Néill belonged to Áed son of Ainmire, although he was not king of Tara: this passed to another Báetán, son of the Nainnid who had taken part in the battle of *Cúil Dreimne*.

At this juncture the Ulaid emerge on the scene. The king-ship of the Ulaid was, in principle, that of the Dál Fiatach; but it is used in a wider sense to mean the overlordship of the whole area east of Lough Neagh, including not only the Dál Fiatach but also the Dál nAraide or Cruithin, and the Dál Riata. In this latter sense it will be designated the kingship of Ulidia.

The traditional boundaries of the over-kingdom of the Ulaid, of the 'province of Conchobor son of Nessa', had been from the river Drowes in the west to the Boyne in the east; the fall of Emain Macha, however, and the com-pression of the Ulaid into the eastern half of the province, had put paid to all probability, if not all hope, of their again dominating the entire province. The position of the tract of land between Carlingford and the Boyne, the plain of Muirtheimne in which the Conaille were later to emerge as a people of some consequence, presents a problem: its inhabitants seem to have been accepted as being of the Ulaid, but as far as the overlordship thereof went, it was apparently a Tom Tiddler's ground.

In the kingship of Ulidia the fifth and sixth centuries are a period of gross darkness. We may conjecture that a period of readjustment to the loss of overlordship of the province, and of Emain, was inevitable, but there is no solid evidence of this. The first ruler of Ulidia of whose existence we can be passably confident is Muiredach Muinderg in the late fifth century, although the date assigned to his death, as with most dates of this period, must be treated with con-siderable reserve. So too the dates of the sons who were believed to have followed him in the kingship. The remain-ing three sons attributed to him, Eógan, Brénaind and Máel Odor, appear as ancestors of later lineages hived off from the main stem of the rulers of the Dál Fiatach.

After the death of Cairell son of Muiredach, the kingship reputedly passed to the king of Dál nAraide, Eochaid son

Fig. 7.

EARLY RULERS OF ULIDIA

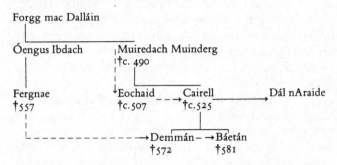

Forgg mac Dalláin

Óengus Ibdach   Muiredach Muinderg
                 †c. 490

Fergnae   Eochaid   Cairell   Dál nAraide
†557   †c.507   †c.525

                        Demmán – → Báetán
                         †572   †581

of Conlae, who was slain in 553: his accession sets a pattern for the future alternation of the kingship of Ulidia between the Dál Fiatach and the Dál nAraide, who themselves were divided into two branches, the main stem and the Uí Echach. The early kings of the Dál nAraide, for what the record is worth, were of the main stem.

After Eochaid son of Conlae, the kingship of Ulidia reverted to the Dál Fiatach, firstly with Fergnae, a nephew of Muiredach Muinderg, then with two grandsons, of whom the second, Báetán, was to prove extremely active. The Dál nAraide were at the time disunited to the extent of bringing the Uí Néill into their internal quarrels in 562/3, when the disputing parties inflicted on one another the battle of *Móin Daire Lóchair* (perhaps Moneymore in Tyrone), the most conspicuous result of which was the loss to the Uí Néill of territory along the western bank of the Bann. Not indeed that the Uí Néill made any great use of their gain: too remote from the bulk of Uí Néill territory to be then adequately controlled, it emerges later as part of the Airgialla. The confusion prevailing within the Dál nAraide is reflected by the report that their king, Áed Brecc, was killed in the battle, along with four other kings of the Cruithin (Dál nAraide); another version held that the king of Dál nAraide, here named Eochaid Láeb, in fact escaped. That there was a dispute for the kingship is obvious; but in the years following the battle, the leading figure among the Dál nAraide would seem to have been Áed Dub son of Suibne, who cannot be placed in the pedigree of the later rulers of Dál nAraide, but who figures both as king and as the slayer of Diarmait, king of Tara, for which he is spoken of by later partisans of the Uí Néill in disobliging terms.

To the north of the Dál nAraide, the Dál Riata was anomalous in having territory both in Ireland and Scotland, on the mainland and the islands. A single dynasty, claiming descent from Fergus Mór son of Erc, ruled on both sides of the North Channel for over a century before any split occurred. The first migration to Scotland, with which Fergus is associated in Dál Riata tradition, would seem to have occurred about the beginning of the sixth century, not improbably with encouragement from the British kingdom of Strathclyde, since the Dál Riata would thereby form a barrier against Pictish attack from the west, and break the lines of communication between the northern and southern Picts. The first half-century or so of their establishment in Scotland seems to have been comparatively peaceful; not until the reign of Gabrán, grandson of Fergus, does there seem to have been any clash with the native Pictish kings, and even this may have been a by-product of his marriage to one Luan, daughter of Brychan, ruler of a British kingdom of Breicheiniog in mid-Scotland. In 558, the year to which Gabhrán's death is attributed, the Picts inflicted a defeat on the Scottish Dál Riata, though whether this took place before or after his death is not known. That this gave the Picts any definable supremacy in other than military terms over the Dál Riata is unclear; but by the end of the third quarter of the sixth century it is probable that Bruide son of Mílchú, king of the Picts, claimed some kind of supremacy over them.

Fig. 8.

EARLY RULERS OF DÁL RIATA

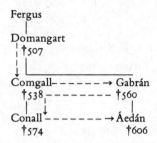

Fergus
|
Domangart
| †507
|
↓ _____
Comgall– – – – – –→ Gabrán
  †538 – – – – – – – – †560
  | | |
Conall – – – – – –→ Áedán
  †574   †606

The lands of the Dál Riata in Ireland were (in theory) under the suzerainty of the king of Ulidia. It is not known whether this position gave rise to any problems during the reign of Gabrán's successor, Conall, who is credited with giving Iona to Columcille. That Bruide son of Mílchú is also credited with the grant is readily explicable on the supposition that he gave his assent as suzerain to the grant. But that Conall recruited Colmán Bec, son of Diarmait and king of Uisneach, as an ally in a warlike expedition in the Hebrides in 568 may be significant, less for any concrete results (which in any case are unknown) than as an indication as to the quarter in which at that time the Dál Riata were looking for allies: among the Uí Néill, rather than among their nearer neighbours the Dál nAraide or the Dál Fiatach.

Conall died in 574. His successor was Áedán son of Gabrán, who at that time was about forty years old. At the time his brother Eóganán probably seemed a more suitable candidate for the kingship, and Áedán's elevation was reputedly brought about by the influence of Columcille, who consecrated him king – allegedly with some reluctance, perhaps because in that year there had been some bloodshed in Kintyre, bloodshed which had some connection with the succession. If this is in fact true, the relations between them must have improved rapidly, for in the following year Columcille acted as intermediary for him at the convention of *Druim Ceit*.

The succession of Báetán son of Cairell to the kingship of Ulidia brought to the surface the tensions latent in the position of the Dál Riata. One of his first steps after the accession of Áedán son of Gabrán was to exact the latter's submission – of which the essential was the giving of hostages – at Island Magee, probably in 574 or early 575. The submission raised a problem: what precisely were the lands of which Báetán thus became suzerain? If it was intended to include the Dál Riata in Scotland, the possibility of a clash with the Picts was obvious. A tightening of Báetán's control over the Dál Riata, which was of some military importance for the men it could muster, and still more for its fleet, equally represented a potential threat for the northern Uí Néill, among whom at this time, although the kingship of Tara was held by Báetán son of Nainnid, the effective power belonged to Áed son of Ainmire of the Cenél Conaill. For Áedán himself, although probably with little choice in the matter, submission to Báetán son of Cairell was none too welcome a posture.

He was fortunate in the presence in his Scottish territory of Columcille: the monastery itself was in some sense the offspring of the benevolence of the rulers of Dál Riata, Columcille himself was largely responsible for Áedán's being vested with the kingship, and most importantly, he was close kin to Áed son of Ainmire.

What preliminary manoeuvrings issued in the convention at *Druim Ceit*, at Mullagh, in Derry, in the summer of 575 are unknown, and the convention itself acquired at a later period a number of legendary accretions which have obscured its real nature. In substance it was an agreement between Áedán son of Gabrán and Áed son of Ainmire that the fleet of the Dál Riata should be regarded as an appurtenance of its Scottish lands – with the implicit consequence that Báetán son of Cairell, or other subsequent kings of Ulidia, would have no claim on it in wartime. Further, it was agreed that the military service of that section of the Dál Riata in Ireland should belong to 'the men of Ireland': a studiously vague phrase, which Báetán son of Cairell, who was not at the convention, nor invited, might interpret if he wished as compatible with his own claims to suzerainty over the Dál Riata. No face would be lost thereby. In reality, Áedán's alliance with Áed son of Ainmire was, and was seen to be, effective insurance against unwelcome attentions on Báetán's part.

Blocked on this side, Báetán turned his attentions elsewhere, to the southwest, in an attempt to colonise the Isle of Man: a risky venture, which took place in two stages, the first in 577, the second in the following year. It is possible that the notion of doing so sprang from the example of the Scottish Dál Riata, whose origins were less than a century old and well known. That it was a success may be doubted, and probably only Báetán's own authority maintained the colony in existence for the remainder of his life. Áedán son of Gabran, on the other hand, secure in his allies of the Uí Néill, was proving more venturesome. In 580/1 he undertook an expedition against the Orkneys; and one or two years after the death of Báetán in 581, he mounted an expedition against Man of sufficient force to induce the Ulidian colony there to abandon it. At the same time he was sufficiently involved with the north Britons, at that time under pressure from the Angles, to have left an unfavourable impression on them: the epithet *bradawc* 'wily' attached to him in Welsh literature suggests that they perhaps found him an unreliable ally. His involvement may have stemmed from his British mother, if report be accurate. There is also some evidence of a clash with the Britons of Strathclyde. To both, however, the Angles of Northumbria, then busily consolidating their power in north-east England, presented a threat, although perhaps of differing degrees of severity, and Áedán found himself involved in resisting them: two of his sons, Domangart and Bran, were killed in 598, apparently by the Angles of Northumbria. In 603 Áedán himself gathered together an army and attacked the Angles. He was defeated by Aethelfrith, king of Northumbria, at *Degsastán* (which is unidentified), with heavy losses, including one Maeluma son of Báetán of the Cenél nEógain, son of one of the holders of the kingship of Tara in the early 570s. The bond with the Uí Néill still held sound.

The Uí Néill 575–605

In the years since the convention of *Druim Ceit*, these latter had had their problems of succession to the kingship of Tara. A necessary preliminary for any successful candidate was the removal of Áed son of Ainmire, and in 580/1 this was attempted by one Colcu, son of the Domnall who died in 566, with unfortunate results for himself, in

Fig. 9.

EARLY RULERS OF CENÉL nEÓGAIN

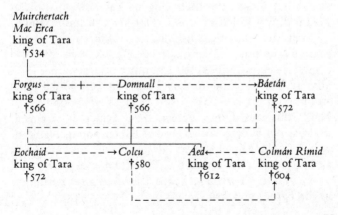

Fig. 10.

EARLY RULERS OF UISNECH

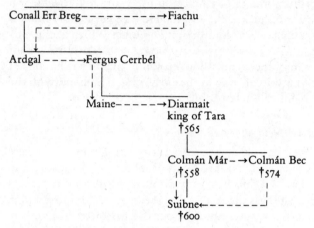

The earlier rulers are very uncertain.

the battle of *Druim Meic Erce* (perhaps Drumhirk in Tyrone). This reverse had the apparent effect of discouraging other ambitious members of the Uí Néill for a few years; but in 586 the then king of Tara, Báetán son of Nainnid, was killed at *Léim in Eich*, by Cummíne, son of Colmán Bec, and one Cummíne son of Librán (apparently a great-grandson of Fergus Cerrbél). Colmán Bec had himself been prominent for a number of years, both as an ally of Conall, king of Dál Riata, in 568, and for an attempt, in 573, to take over the leadership of the Uí Néill; this ended in a defeat, from which he escaped, at *Feimen* in Brega. The slaying of Báetán son of Nainnid, which he instigated, was almost certainly a serious attempt to gain the kingship of Tara. It failed however, and Colmán himself within a year fell to Áed son of Ainmire in the battle of *Belach Dathi*.

Fig. 11.

THE CENÉL CONAILL

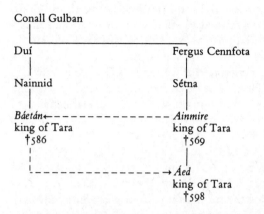

Conall Gulban

Duí — Fergus Cennfota

Nainnid — Sétna

Báetán◄ — — — — — — — — — — — — *Ainmire*
king of Tara — king of Tara
†586 — †569

— — — — — — — — — — — — — — →*Áed*
king of Tara
†598

Áed himself succeeded to the kingship of Tara, and enjoyed a largely undisturbed reign. The Laigin to the south were on the whole quiescent, and their affairs in the second half of the sixth century correspondingly obscure. On the death of Áed Cerr in 591, the kingship of the Laigin passed to Bran Dub son of Eochu, of the Uí Felmeda, a branch of the southern Laigin and it is entirely possible that he was much more interested in keeping an eye on his potential rivals among the Uí Dúnlainge than in pursuing the old grudge against the Uí Néill, against whom he had already proved himself by defeating them in 590 near Cloncurry. Circumstances, however, were to force him onto the offensive: circumstances which, encrusted though they became with later legend, nonetheless seem to boil down to offensive conduct by Cummascach, son of Áed son of Ainmire. The tale later told was that Cummascach, visiting the territory of the Laigin, demanded the right to sleep with Bran Dub's wife, which she was unwilling to concede. Such a type of hospitality appears in the saga literature, which may well arouse suspicions of the story. It seems at least probable that the slaying of Cummascach in 597 was the result of some insult offered to Bran Dub.

Honour demanded that the death be avenged, and Áed is reputed to have refused all offers of compensation. Instead, he invaded and devastated the territory of the Laigin in the following year, 598. The Laigin managed to block him when he had penetrated as far south as *Dún Bolg*, a little to the south of Donard in Wicklow, and inflicted a shattering defeat on him. Áed himself was the principal casualty in the battle, but Béc son of Cuanu, king of the Uí Tuirtri in Airgialla, also fell by the Laigin.

The death of Áed initiated a period of turmoil, which a series of raids by Bran Dub into Brega in 600 no doubt did little to calm. Among the southern Uí Néill, the chief contenders for the succession to Áed were Suibne, son of the Colmán Már who had been slain in 558, and his uncle, Áed Sláine son of Diarmait. Both, considering that most people were lucky to reach the age of forty, must have been of comparatively advanced age at the time. Matters between them were settled temporarily by Áed's slaying Suibne in 600. Among the northern Uí Néill, the contest lay between Colmán Rímid, king of Cenél nEógain, and Conall, son of the late Áed, and it was resolved – again, temporarily – by Colmán's victory over the latter in 601/2 near Lough Slevin in Westmeath. An observer at the time might have expected as a logical development of the situation yet another contest, between Colmán and Áed Sláine; in fact, this did not occur. Instead, the two seem to have come to an agreement to share the kingship of Tara between them. Like all such arrangements, it was intrinsically unstable; but its lack of stability had no time to come to the surface, for in 604 both Colmán and Áed Sláine were killed, the first by one Lóchán Dílmana of his own people, the second by Conall Guthbind, son of the Suibne whom Áed had slain in 600. The actual killing was the work, not

EARLY RULERS OF THE UÍ CEINNSELAIGH

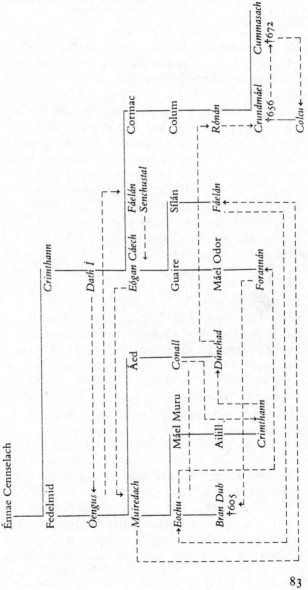

The earlier rulers are far from certain.

83

of Conall Guthbind, but of his fosterbrother, Áed Guastan, and one Báegal Bile.

An obvious candidate for the succession was Conall Cú, son of Aed son of Ainmire; but any possibility of this was eliminated by his death in the same year. The successful candidate was Áed Uairidnach, of the Cenél nEógain, son of the Domnall who died in 566; and he signalised his accession by defeating, in 605, Bran Dub and the Laigin at *Slaebre*. Bran Dub survived the battle itself, but was slain in the same year by one of the Laigin – allegedly one Sarán Saebderc, his own son-in-law, and superior of the church of *Senboth Sine* in the territory of the Uí Ceinnsealaigh; another version of the circumstances of his death places it in the battle of *Damcluain* (perhaps near Templeshanbo in Wexford) fought among the Laigin themselves. There is not sufficient evidence for opting for one or the other version.

The South and Connacht to 602

Of affairs elsewhere in the country during the late decades of the sixth century very little is known. The Osraige, who functioned more or less as a buffer state between the Laigin and the rulers of Cashel, were at the time ruled by a dynasty not of the Osraige themselves, but by a branch of the Corco Loígde of Munster known as the Uí Duach Argatrois. The first recorded was one Cúcraide son of Duí, of the mid-sixth century; a daughter of his, Mugain, was allegedly one of the wives of Diarmait son of Fergus Cerrbél, king of Tara, and he himself is claimed as a close friend of Ciarán of Seir, whose mother was of the Corco Loígde. He seems to have been succeeded by his brother Feradach, who was slain on his sickbed by the Osraige themselves in 582. This seems to have been one of the continuing attempts by the native Osraige to rid themselves of their Corco Loígde overlords, but if this is so, it failed in its object, since Feradach was apparently

Fig. 13.

RULERS OF CASHEL TO 637.

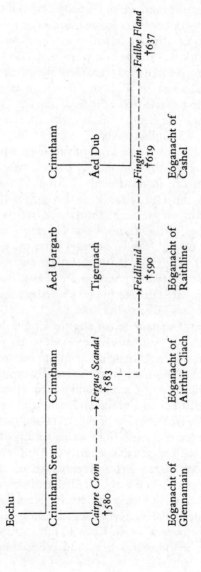

| Eóganacht of Glennamain | Eóganacht of Airthir Cliach | Eóganacht of Raithline | Eóganacht of Cashel |

Eochu

Crimthann Srem — Crimthann

Cairpre Crom †580 — → Fergus Scandal †583

Áed Uargarb

Tigernach

→ Feidlimid †590

→ Fingin †619

Crimthann

Áed Dub

→ Failbe Fland †637

succeeded by his son Colmán, who figures as a friend and patron of Cainneach of Aghaboe, who died in 599 or 600. It seems probable that he was succeeded by one Cennfáelad, of whom nothing is recorded save his paternity of Scandlán, the last king of this line to rule the Osraige: the latter's death took place in 643, and a contemporary and namesake, Scandlán son of Colmán, seems to have succeeded in expelling the Corco Loígde dynasty in his own favour – although the identity of names has caused some confusion. A son of Scandlán son of Cennfaelad, one Illand, was killed in 656, possibly as a kind of mopping up operation.

Affairs in the kingship of Cashel, west of the Osraige, are equally ill-documented. After Óengus son of Nad Fraích and Duí Iarlaithe at the end of the fifth and the beginning of the sixth century, for well over half a century nothing is known, until one Cairpre Crom, reputedly a grandson of Óengus, emerges from the mist in 573 as the alleged victor in a battle at *Femin*, near Cashel, of which the historicity and location are at best dubious. Cairpre's death is dated in 580, and his successors alternated between the various Eóganachta lines.

Over the Shannon, among the Connachta, the late sixth century shows already the dynastic pattern of the following centuries. The Uí Ailella, claiming descent from Ailill son of Eochu Mugmedon, are politically of slight significance; the kingship had become, and was to remain, the possession of the Uí Briúin and the Uí Fiachrach, themselves divided into the Uí Fiachrach of the north and the Uí Fiachrach of Aidne, in the south. The earliest king of the Connachta dated with reasonable security is Ailill Inbanda, reputedly a son of Eógan Bél and grandson of Duí Galach, and hence one of the early Uí Briúin; but there is, and was, much confusion over the precise parentage of Eógan Bél, since he is alternatively alleged, among other parentages, to have been a son of Cellach, son of Ailill Molt, king of Tara and himself a grandson of ·Fiachra. By this latter reckoning he was therefore one of the early Uí Fiachrach. In effect, nothing is known of the kin of Ailill Inbanda. His successor as ruler of the Connachta was believed to be Eochu Tirmcharna, ancestor of the later Uí Briúin dynasty, but this remains as doubtful as his reputed successors, Feradach son of Ros of the Uí Fiachrach, and Feradach's grandson Máel Chothaid. The vagueness and confusion of the sources not improbably reflect, wittingly or not, the state of affairs at the time, with Uí Briúin and Uí Fiachrach contending indecisively for supremacy. With the rule of Áed son of Eochu Tirmcharna we come to somewhat firmer ground. There is some reason to believe that he had already gained ascendance among the Connachta by 561, when he took part in the battle of *Cúil Dreimne*. He was slain in 577, allegedly by the Uí Briúin themselves – possibly by dissidents among them – and succeeded by his son Uatu, who managed to survive for almost a quarter of a century, dying in 601/2.

Ulidia to 629

The affairs of Ulidia are slightly better documented. After the death of Báetán son of Cairell in 581, the overlordship

Fig. 14.

RULERS OF THE DÁL nARAIDE TO 626

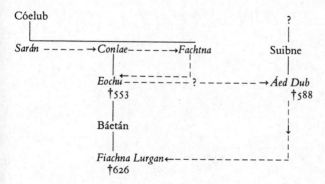

passed from the Dál Fiatach to the Dál nAraide, in the person of Áed Dub son of Suibne; in 588 he was killed by another member of the Dál nAraide, one Fiachna Lurgan son of Báetán, who was to enjoy some reputation as a collector of relics, and whose rule was to span more than three decades. He accession may well have been favoured by a dearth of able candidates from the Dál Fiatach, as well as by the support of the Dál Riata, under Áedán son of Gabrán, who was happy to support any power likely to counterbalance the power of the Dál Fiatach. There seems at least to have been no opposition from the Dál Fiatach for some two decades, and the earliest clash with others of which there is record was with the Cianachta of Brega to the south, under Gerrthide son of Crónán, at *Eudann Mór* in Brega in 594, in which Fiachna was the victor. In this case, Fiachna was the aggressor. Within Ulidia itself, the first open clash recorded came at *Cúl Caíl* (perhaps Kilkeel in Down) in 601, where he inflicted a defeat on another Fiachna, son of Demmán, of the Dál Fiatach. The latter was reputed to have been married to Fiachna Lurgan's sister Cuimne Finne, who bore him two sons, Suibne and Mael-coba, though to what period of his life this is to be referred is not clear; he was also reputed to.have been married to

Fig. 15.

RULERS OF DÁL RIATA 606–642

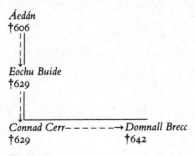

Áedán
†606

Eochu Buide
†629

Connad Cerr— — — — — —→*Domnall Brecc*
†629   †642

one Cuimne Duibe, daughter of Furudrán, king of Uí Tuirtre.

For over twenty years after the battle of *Cúl Caíl* there is, oddly, no trace of further clashes between the two. The change of king and dynasty, when it comes, occurs abruptly and without warning, in 626. In that year, Fiachna son of Demmán succeeded in defeating Fiachna Lurgan at Knocklayd in Antrim. The latter's death rendered it a decisive victory, but the second Fiachna was not long destined to savour its fruits. In the following year, at *Ard Corann*, Fiachna fell to a combination of the Dál nAraide and Dál Riata: the latter were commanded by Connad Cerr, son of the king of Dál Riata, whose sister is reputed to have been the mother of Congal Cáech, king of Dál nAraide.

The close links between Dál Riata and Dál nAraide which functioned so satisfactorily at *Ard Corann* proved less fortunate for the Dál Riata than for the Dál nAraide. On the death in 629 of Eochu Buide, who had followed Áedán son of Gabrán in the kingship, Connad Cerr succeeded him as king of Dál Riata in both Ireland and Scotland, but lasted only a few months: he found himself involved in the internal quarrels of the Dál nAraide. Congal Cáech, become king of Ulidia, seems to have opted out of the problems of the Dál nAraide, and was succeeded as king of these latter by Máel Caích son of Scandal; not, however, without some opposition from others, most notably Dícuill son of Eochu, king of the subordinate kingdom of Cenél Cruithen. The latter, with assistance from the Dál Riata, contested the succession, and in so doing fell in the battle of *Fid Eoin* in 629. With him fell Connad Cerr, Rígullán, a grandson of Áedán, and Fáilbe, a son of the late Eochu Buide, along with a number of Northumbrian soldiers of fortune. Connad's successor was his brother, Domnall, who proved to have a talent for disaster.

While the Ulaid were thus occupied, the Uí Néill were attempting to grapple with similar problems. Áed Uaridnach, after his defeat of Bran Dub king of Laigin at *Slaebre* in 605, enjoyed a quiet reign as king of Tara, and died in 612. Conall 'Laeg Breg', son of Áed Sláine, seems to have had ambitions to become king of Tara, but was defeated and killed in the same year by Óengus son of Colmán, in the battle of *Odba* (perhaps near Navan in Meath). Óengus son of Colmán was brother to the king of Uisneach, but seems to have been content to remain so; a son of Colmán Már, who was killed in 558, he must have been, by contemporary standards, an old man, though clearly a vigorous one. From the intrigues which must have followed, and no doubt preceded, the death of Áed Uaridnach, one apparent winner seems to have emerged: Mael Coba, son of Áed son of Ainmire, of the Cenél Conaill. He was, however, challenged and defeated in the battle of 'Bessy Bell Mountain' (Sliab Truim) in Tyrone in 615 by Suibne Menn son of Fiachna, of the Cenél Feradaig branch of the Cenél nEógain. Suibne seems to have had the military assistance of the Luigne, and could perhaps call on some of the Airgialla through his marriage to Rónait, daughter of Dúngalach, king of Uí Tuirtre. He seems to have remained unchallenged in the kingship of Tara for over a decade.

The affairs of the Airgialla, under pressure from the Cenél nEógain and transmitting this pressure eastwards to the Ulaid, are obscure. Within this loose confederation of kingdoms there emerge, occasionally, more or less dominant figures: so Bécc of the Uí Tuirtre, slain in 598, figures as king of the descendants of Colla Uais, that is, the northern Airgialla, as does his son Furudrán (†645) and Furudrán's son Máel Dúin (†662); all three are in later sources described as kings of the Airgialla, which means no more than that they enjoyed an undefined pre-eminence rather than a formal overlordship.

Since Suibne was of the northern Uí Néill, a free field was left to the southern Uí Néill to contest the lesser, but still appetising, kingship of Uisnech. After the slaying of Suibne son of Colmán Már this had passed to his brother Fergus: this latter was in 618 slain by one Anfartach grandson of Mescán, who is otherwise unknown, and who can hardly have been hoping to replace Fergus himself in the kingship. The killing may have been prompted by some private grudge. In fact, Fergus' successor was his brother Óengus, who had distinguished' himself in the battle of *Odba* in 612; he enjoyed some three years of rule before being killed in 621 by one Domnall son of Murchad, whose background and motives are as obscure as those of Anfartach. It is tempting to associate him with the branch of the southern Uí Néill focussed around the sons of the late Áed Sláine, who were bitterly opposed to the ruling dynasty, and were at the time engaged in establishing a fresh dynasty of their own in Brega – one unfortunately (from their point of view) less prestigious than that of Uisnech. Associated with them may have been the descendants of Illand, son of Conall Err Breg, who appear fleetingly in southern Uí Néill politics from time to time.

Certainly the succession to Óengus was not settled without bloodshed: a battle at *Cenn Deilgthen* in Meath in 622 proved the only satisfactory means of choosing a successor, and from it Conall Guthbind, son of Suibne, emerged victor, with the assistance of Domnall Brecc of the Dál Riata. The chief casualties on the losing side, of which the identity is ill-defined, were two grandsons of Illand.

The Laigin 605–633

The affairs of the Laigin at the same period, in contrast, were comparatively peaceful. Bran Dub had been succeeded as king of the Laigin, not by another member of the southern Laigin, but by Rónán son of Colmán, of the

Uí Dúnlainge. His reign, entirely uneventful as far as we know, ended with his death in 624; and he was succeeded by a son of Áed Cerr, one Crimthann of Cualu. There is some reason to suppose that this latter was not unopposed by the Uí Dúnlainge, more particularly by Rónán's brother Fáelán; but this latter had other problems to cope with, more particularly the aggressiveness of the Uí Ceinnselaig under their leader Crundmáel 'Bolg Luatha'. Crimthann of Cualu may have been accepted as a stop-gap: the Uí Néill to the north seem to have deemed him no particular threat to them, turning their attention rather to Crundmáel in 626, in what seems to have been a somewhat indecisive clash. Fáelán son of Colmán in turn clashed with him two years later, in 628, at *Duma Aichir*, also with indecisive results. By the time of Crimthann's death in 633, however, Fáelán had achieved sufficient predominance in the province to be accepted as king of the Laigin.

In the meantime, on the western flanks of the Laigin,

Fig. 16.

RULERS OF UÍ FAILGI TO THE END OF THE 7th CENTURY

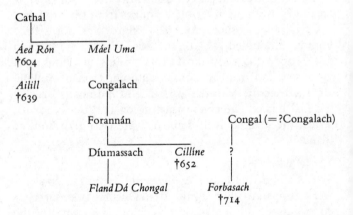

The exact sequence after Ailill cannot be determined.

the Uí Failgi were beginning to emerge as a people of some importance. The succession of their rulers in the late sixth and early seventh centuries is obscure, although the dubious testimony of the annals and regnal lists is to some extent supplemented by a few lines of verse on the fort of the kings of Uí Failgi at Rathangan, in Kildare. The earliest recorded is one Bruidge, whose death took place in 579; the next recorded is Áed Rón, who was killed in 604 at Loughsewdy in Westmeath, apparently while inter-meddling with the affairs of the men of Meath and Brega; and he seems to have been succeeded by his son Ailill, who survived until 639. The brothers of Áed Rón, potential rulers though they were, appear in the record only as ancestors of later subdivisions of the Uí Failgi: Áed Rón himself as ancestor of the Uí Cormaic, Máel Uma as ancestor of the Uí Flaind, Coibdenach of the Uí Móenaig and Uí Máel Umae, and Óengus Berraide as ancestor of the Uí Berraide. Of these, only the Uí Flaind were to have a future as rulers of the Uí Failgi.

Munster and Connacht 601–629

Of affairs in the kingdom of Cashel there is little to record: if there was any annalistic activity there, it has not survived in any identifiable quantity, and those who compiled such records elsewhere rarely go further than noting the death of a king of Cashel, most of whom seem to have died peacefully in their beds. All that emerges from these is that the succession thereto alternated, with some seeming impartiality, between the various branches of the Eógan-achta [Fig. 13].

Matters in Connacht, by contrast, are rather more lively. On the death of Uatu son of Áed as king of Connachta in 601/2, it seems that the Uí Briúin were unable to conjure forth a sufficiently forceful candidate for the kingship: it went, by default, to Colmán son of Cobthach, of the Uí Fiachrach of the south. The Uí Fiachrach of the north were at the time in no position to put forward an alternative candidate, assuming they felt inclined to do so, since they were under pressure from the Cenél Cairpre, who in 602 administered a defeat to Máel Cothaid, king of the Uí Fiachrach, at Aughris in Sligo. The aggressiveness of the Cenél Cairpre may have been encouraged to some extent by the northern Uí Néill in the hope of extending the area of their suzerainty, and the Cenél nEógain, for example, may well have been actively involved with the Cenél Cairpre. This, if so, would account for the involvement of such persons as Ailill son of Báetán of the Cenél nEógain in Cenel Cairpre affairs: he died by violence at *Mag Slecht* in Cavan in 620.

Such conjectural pressures apart, Colmán's reign seems to have been uneventful; but its surface placidity is probably deceptive. The Uí Briúin, under Rogallach son of Uatu, ended his reign violently in 622, in the battle of Canbo in Roscommon in which Colmán himself fell. As might be expected, Rogallach himself succeeded to the kingship of Connacht.

In the early years of Rogallach's rule, a son of Colmán, Guaire of Aidne, was beginning to make some slight name for himself. He had become obscurely involved in Munster affairs, and found himself on the losing side in the battle of Cahernarry in Limerick, against Faílbe Flann, king of Munster; with him in his discomfiture were Conall son of Máel Dub, probably of the northern Uí Fiachrach, and the king of Uí Maine, who was killed in the battle. It was one of the rare intrusions of the Connachta into Munster affairs, effectively separated as they were by the Shannon, and it has been suggested that it was essentially an attempt to recover from the kingdom of Cashel the land south of Slieve Aughty, which had once been part of the territory of the Connachta, and was now occupied by the Dál gCais. For the time being, at any rate, Guaire presented no serious threat to Rogallach.

Within the Uí Néill, a contender for the kingship of Tara had by the late twenties emerged: Domnall son of Áed, of the Cenél Conaill, in opposition to the incumbent Suibne Menn of Cenél nEógain. By 628 matters had become sufficiently tense to issue in a battle between the two at *Both* (probably Raphoe in Donegal), in which Domnall was defeated and put to flight. In the same year however Suibne was attacked by the Ulaid under Congal Cáech son of Scandal at *Traig Bréni* on the shore of Lough Swilly, defeated and killed. Whether there was any collusion between Domnall and Congal is unclear: Congal was later reputed to have been Domnall's foster son, which would be an entirely adequate reason for coming to his aid, but the tale rests on shaky foundations. The death of Suibne, however, removed the major obstacle to Domnall's accession to the kingship of Tara, which he signalised by invading and devastating the territory of the Laigin – evoking, however, no recorded response from the Laigin, who were at the time preoccupied with the perennial dispute between the northern and southern Laigin.

In the following year, 629, he turned on Congal Cáech, and inflicted a defeat on him at *Dún Cethirn* in Antrim, with the loss on his own side of Guaire son of Forannán, king of the Uí Fiachrach of Ardstraw. The antecedents of this attack are obscure: later legend, which may have some slight basis in fact, alleged that Congal Cáech had been alienated from Domnall by an insult, of which details are given with the precision appropriate to fiction. There may be something in it. At any rate, Domnall's victory on this occasion – although Congal survived to fight another day – served to give notice of his supremacy in the north.

Within the northern Uí Néill, his survival seemed assured in any case by the conflicts splitting the Cenél nEógain. In the battle of *Leitheirbe*, in 630, between the descendants of Muirchertach Mac Erca, led by Máel

Fithrich son of Áed Uaridnach, and those of Feradach, led by Suibne Menn's brother Ernáine, the latter emerged victorious, but to all appearances presented no real threat to Domnall's position. Ernáine himself died in 636; and Domnall had moreover a vigorous supporter in the north in Conall Cáel, son of Máel Coba, Domnall's brother, who defeated the Cenél nEógain in the battle of *Sailtine*, in 637. In the same year Domnall defeated the Ulaid in the battle of Moira, in Down. Later legend to the contrary notwithstanding, the attack in this case almost certainly came from Domnall, although in so doing he may well have been anticipating Congal's own intentions, since the latter had recruited Domnall Brecc, king of Dál Riata, as an ally. Whether Domnall Brecc was actually present at the battle or not, his men were; although his support may have been due not only to the traditional friendship of Dál Riata and Dál nAraide, but also to his friendship with Conall Guthbind son of Suibne, whom he had supported in the battle of *Cenn Deilgthen* and who had been slain in 635 by the sons of Áed Sláine; for these ranked as the chief supporters of Domnall son of Áed among the southern Uí Néill.

The battle of Moira proved as disastrous for Congal Cáech as for the men of Dál Riata. Congal himself perished in the battle; and for the Dál Riata, it was another misfortune to add to that which they had already suffered in 634 at *Calathros* (probably in Islay), and were to suffer again in 638 at the hands of the Picts in *Glenn Mureson*. Domnall Brecc himself met his death four years thereafter, at the hands of Owain, king of the Britons, in the battle of Strathcarron in Stirlingshire; and for all practical purposes his death marks the end of the Scottish-Irish kingdom of Dál Riata. Domnall Brecc's successors, whose obscure and confused succession is a sound guide to the state of their kingdom, attempted to ride two horses simultaneously for some time longer; but from about the middle of the seventh century the Irish Dál Riata goes in effect its own separate way.

Domnall son of Áed died a natural death in January, 642. Later confusion over the identity of his successor no doubt reflects the situation at the time. Both Cellach and Conall Cáel, sons of Mael Coba, were reputed to be his successors, but this was probably among the northern Uí Néill only; among the southern Uí Néill, Diarmait and Blathmac, two sons of Áed Sláine, had some support.

As far as the southern Uí Néill were concerned, the preceding years had in any case been such as to cause confusion. After Crimthann, king of the Laigin, had in 633 been defeated and slain in the battle of *Áth Goan*, on the western reaches of the Liffey, by a combination of Fáelán son of Colmán of the Uí Dúnlainge, Faílbe Flann king of Cashel and Conall Guthbind, king of Uisnech, the latter felt sufficiently secure to tackle the threat posed, at least potentially, by the sons of Áed Sláine. Two of them, Congal, king of Brega, and Ailill the Harper, he killed in 634: a false move, for it might well have been better to let sleeping dogs lie. In the following year, another son of Áed Sláine, one Diarmait Ruanaid, struck back at Conall, with the aid of Máel Umai son of Forannán of the Airgialla, and slew him. Conall's death thus left Diarmait probably the most powerful man among the southern Uí Néill; but he seems to have had no ambition to take over the kingship of Uisnech, which passed to Conall's brother Máel Doid. The latter ended a long and obscure reign peacefully in 654. The object of Diarmait's manoeuvrings was plainly enough the kingship of Tara, which during the rule of Domnall son of Áed he was unlikely to achieve. After Domnall's death, Diarmait emerges only gradually from the years of confusion. His defeat of Guaire of Aidne, king of Connacht, in 649 in the battle of *Carn Conaill* (Ballyconnell in Galway), no doubt enhanced his prestige; and among the northern Uí Néill, disputes took a bitter turn in 650 with the battle of *Dún Cremthainn*, in which Óengus son of Domnall was defeated and killed by Cellach and Conall Cáel. Within the southern Uí Néill, it seems probable that the adherents of Suibne's son could count on some support from the Laigin; if so, they may account for the slaying in 651 of two sons, Dúnchad and Conall, of Blathmac son of Áed Sláine, by one Máel Odrán of the Laigin in his mill. A non-political motive for the killing cannot however be ruled out.

Competition from the northern Uí Néill took another blow in 654, when Diarmait succeeded in killing Conall Cáel; about the same time, probably, he also captured Cellach, who died four years later in captivity in *Brugh na Bóinne*. Thereby, all immediate competition of any substance from the northern Uí Néill was eliminated. Others, within the southern Uí Néill, may however have had ambitions: in the battle of *Ogoman*, in 662, Blathmac suffered a defeat, in which one Conaing, a grandson of Áed Sláine, fell, along with Ultán son of Ernáine, king of the Cianacht of Brega, and Cennfáelad son of Gerthide, also of the Cianachta. Perversely, however, the victor remains anonymous.

The Laigin and Munster 633–666

In the south of the country, at the same period, obscurity is still the rule. The removal of Crimthann of Cualu in 633 made it clear that the dominant figure among the Laigin was Fáelán son of Colmán; his dominance however was not unchallenged by the Uí Ceinnselaigh, with whom he clashed in 645, though no decisive result either way is recorded. A further clash is recorded two years later, in 647, which in all probability was a piece of muscle-flexing by Colcu, son of Crundmáel, king of the Uí Ceinnselaig. The remainder of Fáelán's rule as king of the Laigin was uneventful, punctuated only by his defeat and slaying of Fáelán, king of the Osraige, in 660. This latter kingdom, recently disembarrassed of its former ruling dynasty of the Corco Loígde, seems to have had little part to play in the wider politics of the south at this period, and it is impossible to establish precisely who were its rulers in the second half of the seventh century. The same problem attaches to the Uí Failgi, in the lists of whose rulers there seems to be a gap at the same period. The last dated ruler of these was one Cillíne son of Forannán, who was slain on a foray into Meath in 652; his probable successor was one Máel Dúin, of whom, typically, nothing is known. It is eminently likely that a great deal of confusion was occasioned by the plague epidemic of 664–6, in which a great many then notable persons perished: Blathmac and Diarmaid in Tara, Fáelán among the Laigin, Cú cen Máthair in Cashel, to name only four. In this latter kingdom, also, almost nothing is known of events except the succession of rulers.

Connacht 629–663

Among the Connachta, in contrast, a certain amount of light is available. It focusses mainly on the figure of Guaire of Aidne, who succeeded to the kingship of Connacht after the death in 649 of the Uí Briúin king of Connacht, Rogallach son of Uatu. Rogallach was in fact slain by one Máel Brigte, son of Mothlachán and the obscure Corco Cullu: whether Guaire instigated this or not, he profited by it, although it is not altogether clear that he assumed the kingship of Connacht immediately on Rogallach's death: some sources claim Guaire's brother Laidcend as Rogallach's successor, and date his death in 656. Some indication of the complication and confusion of the sources for the period is the report in one text that Laidcend's wife Deog later married Guaire, and was a daughter of Fíngin son of Áed, the king of Cashel who died in 619. To complicate matters further, Guaire is also alleged to have married Órnait, daughter of Cúán son of Amalgaid, a later king of Cashel who died in 641; she in turn is alleged to have previously been wife to Sechnusach, son of Fíngin, and to have borne him three sons. All these reports may in fact be true: in marital complications the seventh century need yield nothing to the twentieth.

Whether Guaire in fact succeeded Rogallach immediately or not, he was beyond doubt the most powerful man among the Connachta on Rogallach's death. The Uí Briúin did not of course acquiesce in the transfer of power to the Uí Fiachrach: in 653 Máenach son of Baíthín, king of Uí Briúin, with the assistance of Cennfáelad son of Colcu, ruler of the lesser kingdom of Uí Briúin Seola, inflicted a defeat on Marcán son of Tomán, king of Uí Maine and Guaire's son-in-law and ally. But these did not constitute in themselves a serious challenge; a more serious challenger was Muirgius, son of Rogallach, and in 654 the Uí Fiachrach of Aidne—which in effect means Guaire—killed him, along with one Fergus son of Domnall and one Áed of Bethra, both sufficiently prominent to have their deaths noted, neither sufficiently notorious to be now identifiable with any certainty.

From at least 656 onwards, then, Guaire was king of Connacht. Notwithstanding his pre-eminence, he failed, from the point of view of the Uí Fiachrach, in one essential in leaving behind no son or brother forceful enough to step into his shoes; and on his death in 663 the rule passed back to the Uí Briúin.

The rule of Ulidia 637–674

Among the Ulaid at this period the Dál Fiatach were enjoying a fresh lease of power. The death of Congal Cáech in the battle of Moira in 637 had proved an uncovenanted bonus for them, and the kingship of Ulidia was promptly seized by Dúnchad son of Fiachna, who ruled until 644, and was then succeeded, peacefully, it appears, by his brother Máel Coba. The latter, however, was slain in 647 by his nephew, Congal Cennfota son of Dúnchad. The motive for this killing is unclear, since Congal seems to have been in no position to succeed Máel Coba in the kingship, which in fact passed to his son Blathmac. The latter enjoyed a long and uneventful reign, punctuated only towards the end by a clash with the Dál nAraide at *Fertas* (near Belfast) in 668; the Dál nAraide, under their king, Cathasach son of Luirgéne, were defeated.

Blathmac died in 670, leaving the way open for Congal Cennfota. It is possible that Congal had some support from the Uí Néill, since his daughter was married to Fínnechta Fledach, king of Tara. He lasted only a short time, until 674, when he was killed by Bécc of Bairche, who clearly, whether his motive was political or private (or both), was at the time in no position to step into Congal's shoes and preserve the overlordship of Ulidia for the Dál Fiatach. The kingship passed in fact to the Dál nAraide under Fergus son of Áedán, who must have been of advanced years, since his father had died in 616. The position is however extremely confused; the king of Dál nAraide at the time belonged to a different branch from Fergus, who was of the Uí Echach (which was nonetheless of the Dál nAraide) and may have been a compromise candidate.

The church between the two plagues

The period around the great plague of 664–6 is in many ways a climacteric, not least for the devastation it wrought among those most intimately involved in politics in various parts of the country. A literal-minded observer, noting the numbers of rulers who perished in it, might well have been tempted to conclude that justice in rule, which was traditionally expected to avert plagues, was almost non-existent at the time. Later reports, not necessarily exaggerated, put the death-roll at a third of the total population, and the pious attributed it to the hand of God, which, however, spared religious no more than the men of blood who ruled secular society: Féichín of Fore, Ailerán the Wise, Manchán of Lemanaghan, bishops and abbots uncounted perished of it.

At this point, then, it is appropriate to consider the state of the church in Ireland between the two milestones represented by this plague, and that of 549. The latter serves in some degree as a turning point in the history of the church in Ireland: it has been estimated that of the clerics whom later generations thought worth commemorating, or whom they were able to trace, the great majority before

MONASTIC FOUNDATIONS
BETWEEN THE PLAGUES

Tory Island
Moville
Fahan
Magilligan
Drumachose
Kilmacrenon
Derry
Conwal
Raphoe
Church Island
Muckamore
Arboe
Bangor
Drumhome
Drumcliff
Devenish
Inishkeen
Cleenish
Aughris
Ballysadore
Kilnemanagh
Achonry
Fenagh
Assylin
Inishkeen
Tibohine
Annaduff
Emlagh
Dunleer
Balla
Fore
Kilskeer
Termonfeckin
Roscommon
Cong
Trevet
Annaghdown
Lemanaghan
Cloonowen
Durrow
Clondalkin
Clonfert
Rahan
Lynally
Lorrha
Birr
Kilmacduagh
Glendalough
Tuamgraney
Roscrea
Timahoe
Aghaboe
Freshford
Leighlin
Leamakevoge
Kilkenny
Ferns
Kilmallock
Ardfert
Ardfinnan
Lismore
Aghadoe
Innisfallen
Clashmore
Cloyne
Skellig Michael
Ross Carbery

0   80Kms
0   50Mls

549 were bishops; between 549 and 600, bishops drop to less than half of those recorded; and between 600 and the great plague, twice as many abbots are thought worthy of record as bishops.

This was the period of the great monastic foundations. Not indeed that some had not been founded at an earlier date: Énda had set up in Aran a school of monasticism which was to become famous, Ciarán had founded Clonmacnois on its sandy ridge overlooking the Shannon, Finnian had founded Clonard, Tigernach Clones, and Colum Terryglass, before 549, in which year these last four died. But from the mid-sixth century onwards the monastic foundations begin to proliferate in a bewildering fashion, and the larger foundations are often surrounded by a *paruchia*, a kind of clientship of lesser churches which either laid claim to having been founded by the founder of the mother church, or had affiliated themselves to this latter.

An excellent example of the ramifications of such monastic federations is afforded by the account of the expulsion in 636 of Mochuda, founder of Lismore, from Rahan in Offaly: this was reputedly occasioned by the dislike of the great monasteries of the Uí Néill, Clonard, Durrow and Clonmacnois, for this intruder into their territory, since Mochuda was of the Ciarraige. On Mochuda's refusing to leave of his own free will, the three communities, of Clonard, Durrow and Clonmacnois, cast lots to decide which of them should venture to lay hands on him; and the lot fell on Clonmacnois. Thereupon the community of Clonmacnois cast lots to settle which of their federation should carry out the expulsion, and the lot fell upon Killeigh; and on Killeigh's casting lots, the final lot fell to Killeigh's subordinate house of *Cluain Congusa*. The chief church of the federation was as a rule that in which the founder's body was buried. The proliferation was made the more easy in that very little was needed to found a church, still less a monastery: two religious

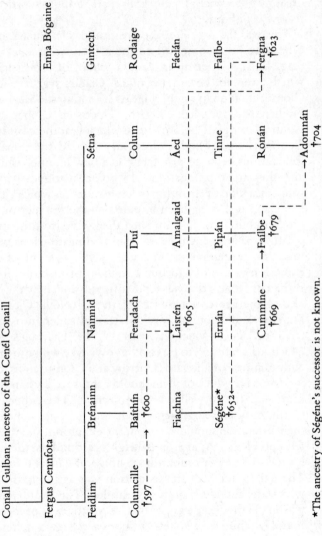

Fig. 17.

THE RULERS OF THE MONASTERY OF IONA TO 704

Conall Gulban, ancestor of the Cenél Conaill

*The ancestry of Ségéne's successor is not known.

104

sufficed for a monastery, neither of whom need be in orders. Daig son of Cairell, the founder of the monastery of Inishkeen who died in 587, is credited with the foundation, almost casually, of half a dozen little monasteries (*monasteriola*). All these seem to have occurred independently of whatever local bishops there may have been, and very often on the patrimony of the founder: of Daig it is recorded that his brothers took a very poor view of his foundation, to the point of attempting to murder him. In other cases, a compromise between the interests of God and the rights of the kin-group seems to have been possible, in that families, while permitting a foundation within their patrimony, might stipulate that, if the line of the founder were unable to provide a suitable candidate, the abbot should be drawn from among themselves, or, quite simply, lay down that the abbot should where possible be one of the *fine griain*, the kin-group which had conceded the land. Probably the best-known example is that of the successive abbots of Iona, all of whom, with one exception whose origins are unknown, belonged to the Cenél Conaill, like the founder of Iona, Columcille, down to the ninth abbot and beyond [Fig. 17].

Such an accommodation to the interests of the secular kin-group was the more possible in that secular society, by the late sixth century, was coming to terms with the Church. The bishop of a *tuath* had been conceded a rank equal to that of the king of a *tuath*. 'Which is the more venerable, king or bishop?' asks a law-text, a little rhetorically, a century later; and replies that 'A bishop is more venerable, for a king rises before him on account of religion; but the bishop, however, raises his knee before a king'—the gesture of an equal. Similarly, the lesser clergy had been conceded status of various degrees of dignity purely by virtue of being clerics: the days when a cleric could be a slave were past. Perhaps also the days when a slave could be a cleric were past: clerics tended now to be persons of some standing in society. Possibly the best example is Columcille, who was kin to the king of Tara and of Cenél Conaill, who felt himself to be of an equality with any man in the country; and his example as a churchman may have given considerable stimulus to the monastic ideal. He himself was a priest and nothing more, and never became a bishop. The integration of the church into Irish society may be symbolised by the appearance among churchmen of former poets such as Colmán son of Lénine, founder of Cloyne, who died in 604, some of whose verse has survived. For their part, and to return the compliment, the churchmen may be responsible for introducing into Irish literature the prose discourse, primarily for homiletic purposes, such as the 'Alphabet of Piety' of Colmán moccu Beógnae of the early seventh century.

The contrast between the monasteries and the household of one of the earlier bishops need not be exaggerated, nor the degree to which the monastic organisation superseded an earlier episcopal organisation. In the seventh century, bishops still continued to act as administrators, and were only gradually and unconsciously ousted by the abbots. In some cases, indeed, there was an attempt to combine the two. At Kildare, in the 630s, the predominant figure was Áed Dub, son of Colmán king of the Laigin; as a bishop, he claimed jurisdiction over all the Laigin, and the monastery itself, under its abbess, was laying claim to a wide *paruchia* of over thirty churches. In the late seventh century, a similar process was taking place in Armagh. There emerges a gradation of bishops similar to that of kings, in which one bishop might have other bishops subordinate to him just as a king might have other kings, each acquiring a proportionately greater honour-price thereby: just as a king of several *tuaths* could thereby lay claim to an honour-price of eight *cumals*, so a 'bishop of bishops' was possessed of an honour-price of eight and two-thirds *cumals*. That of such a high-powered ecclesiastic as the bishop of Emly was equal to that of the king of Cashel.

5 From the great plague to the Vikings (666–c. 800)

The Uí Néill 665–695

Blathmac and Diarmait, joint kings of Tara, died of the pestilence in 665, having seen several sons predecease them: Blathmac's sons Dúnchad and Conall by violence in 651, and Eochaid in 660; while Diarmait's son Cernach had died in 664. But their grip, and that of their adherents, on the kingship of Tara, seems to have been sufficiently firm to allow it to pass, without any notable hindrance, to Blathmac's son Sechnasach. Such possible rivals as the sons of Domnall son of Áed had vanished: two, Conall and Colcu, had been killed in 663 by one Cerrnceinn; another, Ailill Flann Esa, died in 666.

Sechnasach survived as king of Tara for six years, and in 671, at the beginning of winter, was killed by Dub Dúin, king of Cenél Cairpre. Both cause and occasion are obscure. It seems unlikely that Dub Dúin had any hopes of succeeding Sechnasach: the last of his line to hold the kingship of Tara had been Tuathal Maelgarb, some three or four generations previously, and the current generation had as little expectation of emulating him as the Cenél Lóegaire had of emulating their eponymous ancestor. A private grudge seems the most likely explanation. The kingship passed smoothly to Blathmac's brother Cennfáelad, who lasted four years before being slain in 675 by a coming man, Fínnechta Fledach, son of Cennfaelad's uncle, Dúnchad, in the battle of *Aircheltra*.

Fínnechta signalised the beginning of his rule by destroying Aileach, the headquarters, at least symbolically, of the
Cenél nEógain, who under their king Máel Dúin represented the most probable threat to his dominance. In fact
throughout his reign, they offered no overt opposition to
him, possibly realising that he would have no dearth of it
from others in the southern Uí Néill, not counting the
Laigin and the Ulaid. To both these latter, a strong king in
Tara presented an obvious danger. The Laigin, opting for
a pre-emptive strike, crossed the border in 677. Their king,
Fiannamail, a great-grandson of Áed Cerr, had succeeded
to the rule of the Laigin in 666, after the death of Fáelán son
of Colmán, with no obvious opposition from the southern
Laigin. The raid into Meath, however, proved a mis-
calculation on his part: near Lagore they found themselves
blocked by Fínnechta and suffered a defeat, although without any notable casualties. To the north, the kingship of
Ulidia was held by Fergus son of Áedán, but the predominant figure was Bécc of Bairche, of the Dál Fiatach. If
it be true that Fínnechta was married to Conchend,
daughter of the Congal Cennfota whom Bécc had slain in
674, there may well have been some personal antagonism
between them. The first move, however, was made by
Bécc, who followed the precedent set by Fiannamail of the
Laigin by striking into Meath in 679, being blocked by
Fínnechta (this time at Teltown), and also being defeated.
In neither case did Fínnechta attempt to follow up his
victory by pursuing the defeated into their own territory;
but early estimates of his character may be right in assuming
that he was responsible for the death of Fiannamail in 680.
The man who struck the blow was one Fochsechán, of
Fiannamail's own people, but he was rumoured to have
been suborned thereto by Fínnechta.

In 688 he retired into clerical life; and his retirement
coincided with a clash in Meath at *Imlech Pich* between Niall
son of Cernach and Congalach son of Conaing, in which

fell Dub dá Inber, king of the Cianachta of Brega, and Uarchride, king of Conaille. On the face of it, this was no more than a scuffle between two of the descendants of Áed Sláine, Congalach being a great-grandson of Áed Sláine, while Niall was a grandson of the Diarmait, king of Tara, who died in 665; and the latter was the victor, although Congalach escaped by flight. But it is quite possible that it marked the first stage of an attempt to seize the kingship of Uisnech, which in turn might be a stepping-stone to the kingship of Tara. In 689, then, Fínnechta emerged again from clerical life: and the same year witnessed the violent death of the king of Uisnech, Diarmait son of Airmedach, at the hands of yet another descendant of Áed Sláine, one Áed son of Dluthach – although elsewhere Fínnechta

Fig. 18.

RULERS OF UISNECH 600–797

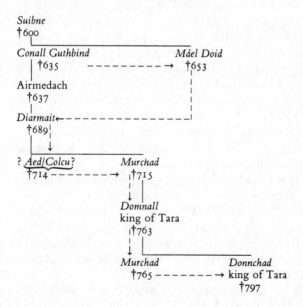

himself is alleged to have been responsible. It is difficult to see what profit it could have brought him, and the fact that Diarmait's son Murchad succeeded him, to all appearances peacefully, which he could hardly have done without Fínnechta's acquiescence, may be thought to argue against the allegation. So too, possibly, does the fact that Fínnechta himself was killed in 695 at *Grellach Dollaig* (perhaps in Louth) by the same Áed son of Dluthach and Congalach son of Conaing in combination. He was succeeded as king of Tara by Loingsech son of Óengus, of the Cenél Conaill. There seems to have been no opposition from the Cenél nEógain, and the southern Uí Néill no doubt had other preoccupations in the quarrelling between the descendants of Áed Sláine and the dynasty of Uisnech.

The Laigin 680–715

Among the Laigin to the south, placidity prevailed. On the assassination of Fiannamail in 680, his place was taken by Bran, grandson of Fáelán, who seems to have prudently abstained from extra-territorial ventures, and to have distinguished himself only by inflicting a defeat on the Osraige in which their king, Fáelchar, was slain. Bran himself died in 695. His successor, Cellach of Cualu, was a man of more commanding calibre. For his wives he ranged far afield: one of them seems to have been of the Cianachta of Glenn Geimin, another, Bé Bail, who died long after Cellach, in 741, was a daughter of Sechnasach, king of Tara. Two others seem to have been drawn from within the Laigin. In the same way, his bestowal of his daughters shows a leaning towards the southern Uí Néill: one, Derborgaill, is claimed as the wife of Fínnechta Fledach, and another, Muirend, who died in 748, was married off to Írgalach of North Brega. Another, Conchend, who died in 743, he married off to Murchad, son of his own pre-decessor Bran son of Fáelán.

While these marriages in some degree constituted

Fig. 19.
RULERS OF THE LAIGIN IN THE SEVENTH AND
EIGHTH CENTURIES
(i) of the Uí Dúnlainge

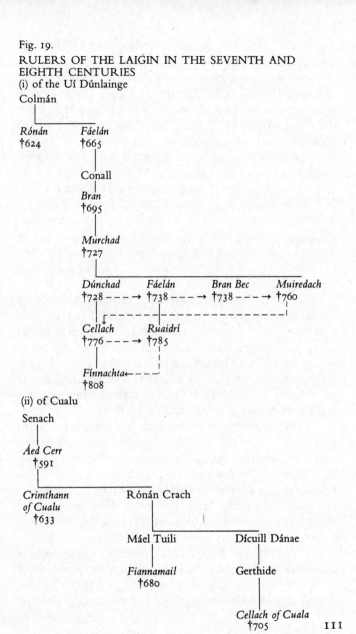

Colmán

Rónán
†624

Fáelán
†665

Conall

Bran
†695

Murchad
†727

Dúnchad   Fáelán   Bran Bec   Muiredach
†728 ----→ †738 ----→ †738 ----→ †760

Cellach   Ruaidrí
†776 ----→ †785

Fínnachta
†808

(ii) of Cualu

Senach

Áed Cerr
†591

Crimthann   Rónán Crach
of Cualu
†633

Máel Tuili   Dícuill Dánae

Fiannamail   Gerthide
†680

Cellach of Cuala
†705

111

insurance against disturbances by the southern Uí Néill, they could not, obviously, provide against the dissensions between the descendants of Áed Sláine. If Cellach, by his daughter's marriage to Írgalach of North Brega, was in some sense an ally of the latter, he was an obvious target for the latter's rivals in south Brega. Niall, son of Cernach Sotal, the most eminent of these, was killed in 701, and his place taken by his son Fógartach. In 704 this latter, with the support of one Bodbchad of Meath, invaded Laigin territory and succeeded in penetrating as far south as Clane in Kildare before being blocked and defeated: Bodbchad was slain, and Fógartach saved himself by flight. A further challenge came in 707, when Congal son of Fergus, now king of Tara, led a hosting against the Laigin, not with any notable success. It may have amounted to no more than showing the flag.

More serious was the problem of the Uí Ceinnselaigh. Under their king, Bran, grandson of Mael Dúin, they were enjoying something of a resurgence of vigour, and in 709 ventured to give battle to Cellach at *Selg* in the neighbourhood of the Glen of Imaal. It is not clear who made the first move to battle, but on the whole the Uí Ceinnselaig are the more likely. In the battle fell two of Cellach's sons, Fiachra and Fiannamail, and many of Cellach's British mercenaries. It is not clear that he was defeated, but neither is it at all clear that he was the winner. It may in fact have been a stand-off. Matters might have gone worse for Cellach thereafter had the southern Laigin not been sufficiently at odds with one another to indulge in a battle at *Áth Buichet* in 712 in which the king of the Uí Ceinnselaigh – still Bran – was slain with his sons, and his kingship taken over by a collateral line.

The recruitment by Cellach of British mercenaries is noteworthy. They came in all probability from the Isle of Man, which apparently served as a refuge after the destruction of the north British kingdom of Rheged, and for some time proved something of a nuisance; they were, for example, responsible for the death of Cellach's son-in-law Írgalach on Ireland's Eye in 702. Service as mercenaries, as an alternative to piracy, had clear advantages for both the Britons themselves and their potential victims; and it is eminently possible that had the Uí Ceinnselaigh also been able to recruit such mercenaries Cellach might not have fared so well in the battle of *Selg*.

Good relations with the men of Meath – or at least the majority of them – seem to have continued until his death. An encounter at *Garbsalach* in Meath, in which Forbasach, king of the Uí Failgi, fell to the men of Meath, was in all probability a modest incursion on his own account. Forbasach himself was the successor of Fland Dá Chongal, who is noteworthy on his own account. More or less contemporary with Cellach of Cualu, though not precisely dated, he also had ranged widely in his marriages. Four of his sons were by Érennach, a daughter of Murchad son of Diarmait, king of Uisnech; four more by an unnamed daughter of one Flann Léna, and yet four more by a girl of doubtful status, who is described as a slave-girl, but linked by blood to the Uí Dúnlainge, from whom Cellach of Cualu's successor was to be drawn. Of these twelve sons, no less than five succeeded him as king of Uí Failgi, though not immediately, since Forbasach was not of his line. To the rulers of the Laigin the Uí Failgi presented as a rule no problem, unlike the Osraige; but these, since the defeat and death of their king Fáelchar in 695, had been, externally at least, quiescent.

Cellach died in 715, and was succeeded in the kingship by his son-in-law, Murchad son of Bran, whose relations with the Uí Néill were to prove less amiable and more aggressive than those of Cellach.

Ulidia 674–714

In the north, the general impression is of quiet, punctuated infrequently by violence. The overlordship of Ulidia was in the hands of the aged Fergus son of Áedán, but he seems to have steered clear of any involvement in quarrels internal or external. From without, the Cenél nEógain, under Mael Dúin son of Máel Fithrich, inflicted a defeat at *Dún Ceithirn* in Antrim on the Dál nAraide and their allies the Cianachta of Glenn Gemin in 681, with the loss to the latter of their kings, Dúngal son of Scandal and Cennfáelad son of Suibne, respectively. The Dál nAraide suffered another loss in the following year, this time at the hands of British pirates, in a battle at Rathmore in Antrim; in this, Cathasach son of Máel Dúin, king of Dál nAraide, was slain. The Dál Riata, for reasons unknown, chose some years later, in 691, to strike southwards and despoil both Dál nAraide and Dál Fiatach.

There is no trace of any participation by Fergus in these events; he died in bed, or at least not in battle, in 692. Of the available aspirants to kingship, Bécc of Bairche, of the Dál Fiatach, was clearly the strongest, and took over the kingship with no recorded opposition. The Dál nAraide seem to have been looking in a different direction, out towards the kingdom of Airthir to the west and southwest of them; they clashed with the Airthir in Farney in 698, with the loss to the Airthir of their king, Conchobor of Macha, and to the Dál nAraide of their own king, Áed Aired. The battle counted, therefore, as a stand-off in so far as neither side won; but in so far as the aggression had in all probability been initiated, on this occasion at least, by the Dál nAraide, it must be counted as a reverse to them.

The main problem confronting Bécc of Bairche at the end of the seventh century was presented not by the Dál nAraide, but by the British pirates who carried out occasional raids from the Isle of Man. These, fortunately, he succeeded in checking in 703 in a battle at *Mag Cuilind* in the Ards, inflicting on them a defeat in which their leader, described as the son of Radgann, was slain. Within the Dál Fiatach he seems to have buttressed his position by marrying Conchend, daughter of Congal Cennfota, perhaps soon after the death of her previous husband, Fínnechta king of Tara, in 694; but he also seems to have made a similar gesture to the Dál nAraide by taking to wife Barrdub, daughter of Lethlobar son of Eochaid Iarlaithe, of the Dál nAraide.

He retired into religion in 707 as a 'pilgrim', dying in 718. An attempt by Cú Chuaráin, king of the Dál nAraide, to take over the kingship of Ulidia lasted no more than a year, since he was slain in 708 by another member of the Dál nAraide; and the rule of Ulidia slipped back into the hands of the Dál Fiatach, under their king, Áed Rón son of Bécc. However, it seemed advisable to discourage the Dál nAraide from again venturing to seize the kingship, and action was duly taken in 709, in *Mag Eilne*, between Bush and Bann, in a battle in which Lethlobar, king of Dál nAraide, was slain, with two of his chief magnates. That this did not settle the matter was shown in 712, when a defeat was inflicted on the Dál Fiatach in which one of Áed Rón's brothers, named Dubthach, was slain: he could well be spared, since Bécc is credited with twelve sons, seven of them by Conchend daughter of Congal Cennfota. The balance was redressed in 714 when two others of Bécc's sons inflicted a defeat on the Uí Echach under their ruler, Eochaid Coba son of Bresal. Thereafter, there was peace for some two decades.

Munster and Connacht 663–742

Throughout this period, the kingdom of Cashel continued to enjoy its accustomed obscurity, save that, dimly perceptible in the scanty sources, the Eóganacht of Loch Léin was rising to prominence, although its time was not yet. Among the Connachta, on the other hand, developments are something clearer. Guaire of Aidne had been succeeded as king of Connacht by one Cennfáelad son of Colgu, of the

Fig. 20.

RULERS OF CASHEL TO 742

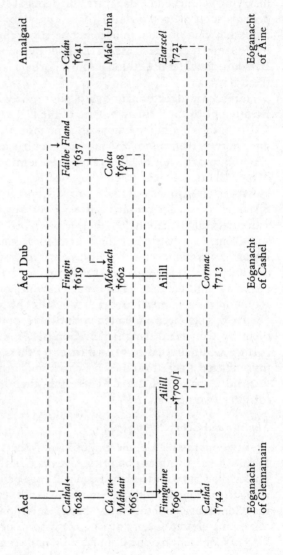

Uí Briúin Seola – the first and only time that this branch of the Uí Briúin attained this eminence. How it happened is matter for conjecture: none of his ancestors, with the dubious exception of Duí Tenga Uma, allegedly his great-great-grandfather, had been king of Connacht, and what claim he possessed to the kingship on these grounds was tenuous in the extreme. He had, however, already established his credentials by his defeat in 653 (admittedly in collaboration with the king of the greater Uí Briúin) of the Uí Maine.

By whatever means he acquired the kingship and contrived to retain it, he survived until 682, when he was slain: by whom is not stated, but it may plausibly be guessed that the Uí Fiachrach of the north were responsible, since the new king of Connacht, Dúnchad of Murrisk, was of that group. With him, the entry of the Uí Fiachrach of the north on the scene marks the start of a new phase in the history of the Connachta in which the Uí Fiachrach of the south, of Aidne, gradually drop out of the running. Dúnchad himself was promptly slain in 683, and neither the killer nor the circumstances are recorded; on the principle of *cui bono* Fergal, grandson of Guaire, may fairly be suspected of having had something to do with the killing, since he succeeded to the kingship.

His reign, however, was no more than a last flare-up of the power of the Uí Fiachrach of Aidne. He died, after what seems to have been quite a peaceful reign, in 696, and his death marks the end of his lineage's intermittent possession of the kingship of Connacht. His successor was of the Uí Briúin, Muiredach Muillethan, son of the Muirgius who had been slain by the Uí Fiachrach of Aidne in 654, although married, if the report be true, to Créd, daughter of Guaire, who had previously been married to Marcán son of Tomáin, king of Uí Maine. The report is doubtful in the extreme, but verification either way is impossible. More plausible is the report of Muiredach's own marriage to Cacht, daughter of the slayer of his grandfather Rogallach.

Muiredach's death in 702 apparently offered no immediate opportunity to the Uí Fiachrach to take over, since the kingship passed immediately to his uncle Cellach, who was of relatively advanced age. His reign was short, but marked by the battle of Corran, in which he inflicted a defeat on Loingsech son of Óengus, king of Tara and of the Cenél Conaill. In this battle, fought at *Claenfhinn*, near the border between the territory of the Cenél Conaill and Connacht, on Saturday, 12 July 704, Loingsech himself was killed with other notables, including Fergus Forcraid, king of Uí Tuirtri. His presence suggests that the clash had its origins in a hosting by Loingsech against the Connachta, and it is possible that there was some connection between the hosting and the affairs of the Cenél Cairpre, who were at this time under pressure from the Uí Briúin, expanding in a north-easterly direction. If these were to succeed in bisecting the Cenél Cairpre (as they ultimately did), the Cenél Conaill would be effectively cut off from participation in the affairs of the southern Uí Néill.

Cellach in any case retired into religious life, and died in 705. Here opportunity seemed to favour the Uí Fiachrach of the north, and Indrechtach, son of Dúnchad of Murrisk, took over the rule of Connacht. He lasted an even shorter time than his predecessor; ironically, he suffered for Cellach's victory in 704, for in 707 Fergal son of Mael Dúin, king of the Cenél nEógain, Fergal son of the late Loingsech, king of Cenél Conaill, and Conall Mend, king of the Cenél Cairpre, succeeded in wiping out the stain of Loingsech's death by killing Indrechtach. The circumstances are not recorded, though there seems to have been no battle of any consequence. It may well be that his Uí Briúin supporters, if any, gave him something less than enthusiastic support. Undoubtedly they profited by his death: their ruler, Indrechtach, a son of Muiredach

Muillethan, succeeded to the kingship and enjoyed a peaceful reign. He seems to have been responsible for one quick foray southwards over Slieve Aughty, in 721, in which one son of Talamnach, of the Corco Baiscind, fell; and with this, honour and prestige were satisfied. The Uí Fiachrach presented no threat to his position, and he seems to have taken life easy, dying on pilgrimage in 723 and being buried in Clonmacnois. The kingship passed peacefully to Domnall son of Cellach, who died in 728, and then reverted equally peacefully to Áed Balb, son of Indrechttach, who ruled until 742.

The Uí Néill 704–728

Among the Uí Néill, the spotlight falls on tensions in Meath. The king of Tara, Loingseach son of Óengus, had fallen in the battle of Corran in 704, and had been succeeded by another notable of the Cenél Conaill, Congal son of Fergus. This latter's reign is noteworthy only for the renewal of hostilities with the Laigin in 707, in which year he devastated their territory, though with what concrete result is not clear; and on his death (of a 'fit', perhaps apoplexy) in 710, the kingship of Tara passed to Fergal son of Mael Dúin, of the Cenél nEogain. His inclinations were more in the direction of expansion eastwards into Airgialla territory, and in 711 he found himself involved in battle at *Sliab Fuait* in Armagh. In this, Tnúthach son of Mochloinges, king of the Airgialla kingdom of Uí Méith fell, along with one Cú Raí son of Áed son of Dluthach, of the descendants of Áed Sláine.

What exactly the latter was doing there, and on whose side, is not known; he would have found just as much action among his own kinsmen. In 712 two of them, Maine son of Niall, and Flann son of Áed, brought their disagreements to the point of battle, in which Maine lost his life. On a larger political scale, the question of the kingship of Uisnech came to the fore in the following year, when

Murchad son of Diarmait, successor to his father on the latter's death in 689, found himself under attack from Flann son of Áed, flushed with his previous success. At Billagh near Kells in 714 the matter was put to the test of battle, in which Murchad, although suffering the loss of two of his chief adherents, of whom one at least was his brother, was able in a counter-attack to defeat and slay Flann and a prominent supporter of his named Dub Dúin grandson of Bécc, whose origins are unclear. For a brief period, Murchad was secure in the kingship, apparently with the support of Fergal son of Máel Dúin, the king of Tara; a prominent opponent of Murchad, Fógartach son of Niall, was expelled by Fergal from the kingship of Brega and driven into exile in Britain. This disorder in Meath seems to have tempted the Uí Failgi in the south to make hay on the borders: the temptation unfortunately proved fatal for their king, Forbasach grandson of Congal, since the men of Meath were sufficiently organised to defeat him at *Garbsalach* in Meath.

Murchad however ruled only a short time after his victory. In 715 he was killed by a brother of Fógartach, one Conall Grant; and in the following year Fógartach was back in the kingship, and made known his return by causing a disturbance at the fair of Teltown in 717, causing two fatalities. In the following year, Conall Grant won a battle at Kells in which fell a number of members of the ruling kin of Uisnech and of their own kin, among whom can be identified two descendants of Conall Guthbind, named Fergal and Amalgaid, and one Gormgal son of Áed son of Dluthach. Two months later, Conall Grant was himself slain by a doubtless exasperated Fergal son of Máel Dúin. The latter seems to have been supporting Domnall, son of the late Murchad, as king of Uisnech, although it is an open question how far he can be regarded in practice as king of Uisnech in the years between his father's death and that of Conall Grant.

In the meantime, the Laigin, under Murchad son of Bran, desirous of profiting by their neighbours' confusion, made a foray into Meath in 719. At Fennor near Slane they were blocked by Fergal son of Máel Dúin, and defeated with the loss of Áed son of Cellach of Cualu; and as tit for tat the Uí Néill proceeded to lay waste portions of Laigin territory no less than five times in that year. Two years later, after a pause to draw breath, the Laigin again struck into Meath, this time in alliance with Cathal son of Finnguine, king of Cashel, and wasted the plain of Brega. On their withdrawal, Fergal gathered together the maximum force then available to him, invaded the territory of the Laigin, and overawed Murchad son of Bran into yielding him hostages. There is some indication that these hostages were intended, not only as security for peace in the future, but also as an earnest of submission. So at least Fergal seem to have interpreted it; and later legend added to this a re-imposition of the mythical *bórama* tribute. It is entirely probable that Fergal held himself entitled to some form of tribute from Murchad, and equally probable that Murchad had no intention of rendering it, and that he did not in fact render anything of the kind.

In consequence, late in the following year (722) Fergal invaded the territory of the Laigin with a large force, apparently in pursuit of what he conceived to be his due; he was given battle by Murchad at the Hill of Allen, in Kildare, on Friday, 11 December. For Fergal it was an unmitigated disaster. The roster of those slain on the side of the Uí Néill leads off with Fergal himself, followed by Conall Menn, king of Cenél Cairpre, Clothgna son of Colcu of the Cianacht, Dub dá Crích son of Dub dá Inber of Ard Cianachta, Flann son of Rogallach of the southern Uí Néill, Áed Laigen of the descendants of Áed Sláine, Nuadu son of Dúnchad of the Cenél Duach, Éicnech son of Colcu king of the Airthir, and one Fergal grandson of Aithechda, of uncertain lineage, but of undoubted eminence. It was a staggering blow, from which the Uí Néill took some time to recover. Murchad seems to have had no inclination to follow up his victory, nor perhaps the ability, for while the reports of the slaughter in the battle are certainly exaggerated, it may reasonably be assumed that the slaughter on the side of the Laigin also was heavy.

Among the Uí Néill themselves, the chief sufferers were those of the north. If the most eminent among those of the south actually took part in the battle (and this is far from certain), they survived it: so with Fogartach, hitherto king of Brega, who took the opportunity to seize the kingship of Tara in succession to Fergal. His brief and unremarkable reign was abruptly terminated by his death in the battle of *Cenn Deilgden* on Saturday, 7 October 724; from this, Cináed son of Írgalach, a great-great grandson of Áed Sláine, emerged as victor, and took over the rule of Tara. No opposition seems to have made itself felt from the northern Uí Néill, the remnants of whom were initially divided among themselves: in 727 the Cenél Conaill—who seem not to have been represented at the battle of Allen— and the Cenél nEógain fought a battle at *Druim Fornocht* in Donegal in which the latter were defeated.

With their pre-eminence among the northern Uí Néill thus established, the Cenél Conaill, under Flaithbertach son of Loingsech, made a successful bid for power in 728 against Cináed son of Írgalach in battle at *Druim Corcain*. Cináed himself was killed there, with Eodus son of Ailill of the Cianacht, and Máel Dúin son of Feradach of the Cenél Lóegaire.

The Laigin 727–738

The repercussions of the battle of Allen were felt equally among the Laigin, though less drastically and less promptly. Murchad son of Bran died in 727, and his death triggered off a struggle for power among the northern Laigin. On the one side seems to have been Etarscél, a son of Cellach of

Cualu, and Congal son of Bran, apparently a brother of Murchad; on the other, Fáelán son of Murchad. The latter was the victor, decisively so, since both Etarscél and Congal were killed in battle at Bairenn; Fáelán however derived no prompt benefit from it, since the political vantage ground among the northern Laigin was at the time held by his elder brother Dúnchad, who in the same year inflicted a defeat on the Uí Ceinnselaigh near Mullaghmast in Kildare, in which fell the king of Uí Ceinnselaigh, Laidcnén son of Cú Mella. Dúnchad thereby became king of the Laigin for the brief period it took for Fáelán to gather supporters to oust him. Within a year, he had succeeded in inflicting a defeat on Dúnchad which the latter outlived by a week; and he himself stepped into Dúnchad's shoes, in more senses than one, since he is alleged to have taken over Dúnchad's wife, Tualaith daughter of Cathal son of Finnguine, king of Cashel. Cathal himself, with Cellach son of Fáelchar, king of the Osraige, is reported to have taken Dúnchad's side in the battle.

Fáelán's new wife may be assumed to have been so without her father's consent, since the latter preserved a vigorous enmity towards the new ruler. In 732 he struck at the southern Laigin, always their most vulnerable point from a Munster point of view, but was defeated by Áed son of Colcu, of the Uí Ceinnselaigh. Three years later hostilities were renewed between the Laigin and Cathal at *Belach Féile*, with heavy losses to the Laigin but heavier losses yet to the men of Munster: Cathal escaped, but lost Cellach son of Fáelchar in the battle. His enemy Fáelán died, unexpectedly, in 738, which was to prove a disastrous year for the Laigin.

The Uí Néill 728–766

Flaithbertach son of Loingsech's accession as king of Tara, had understandably provoked some dissatisfaction among the Cenél nEógain, but there was little that these could immediately do about it. Four years after his accession, however, they were in sufficient fettle to oppose him militarily, and inflicted on the Cenél Conaill a defeat in which fell Flann Gohan, son of the Congal who had preceded Fergal son of Máel Dúin in the kingship of Tara, and a magnate named Flaithgus son of Dub Díberg. Flaithbertach himself seems not to have taken part in the battle, any more than a similar battle in the following year, 733, in *Mag Itha*, in east Donegal, in which another son of Congal, one Conaing, was slain on the side of the Cenél Conaill. Yet again, in 734, occurred another encounter between them in *Mag Itha*, in which the Cenél nEógain seem to have suffered some losses. None of these clashes seem to have been at all conclusive, but Flaithbertach, wearied of defending his position, or perhaps of having it defended for him, quitted the kingship for religion, dying in Armagh in 765.

He was succeeded, without trouble, by Áed Allán, son of Fergal son of Máel Dúin. In 735 Áed proceeded to demonstrate his prowess by inflicting a defeat on the Ulaid in Muirtheimne in which fell Áed Rón, king of Ulidia, and Conchad son of Cuanu, king of the Uí Echach of Cuib. The battle was reputedly occasioned by the profanation of *Cell Conna*, subordinate to Armagh, by a follower of Áed Rón; and for this vengeance was sought by Congus, successor of Patrick and abbot of Armagh.

There remained the question of the Laigin, since his father's death at their hands was as yet unavenged. In enmity to the Laigin, though for other reasons, he had a fellow in Cathal son of Finnguine, king of Cashel; and in 737 he arranged a meeting with him at Terryglass, with results seemingly satisfactory to both. Judging by subsequent events, it was in all probability a treaty of non-aggression, an agreement by Cathal not to interfere in any action Áed might take against the Laigin. In the following year, then, he attacked the Laigin, and brought them to battle at *Áth Senaig* in Kildare on 19 August, inflicting a heavy defeat on them. Áed himself was wounded, but Áed son of Colgu, of the Uí Ceinnselaigh, who had emerged as king of the Laigin, was slain by Áed Allán in single combat. The carnage was heavy: among those listed as slain were Bran Bec son of Murchad, of the Uí Dúnlainge, Fergus son of Móenach and Dub dá Crích great-grandson of Cellach, two lords of the Fothairt, Fiangalach grandson of Máel Aithgén of the Uí Briúin of Cualu (possibly their king), Conall, great-grandson of Aithechdae, of another branch of the Uí Dúnlainge, four sons of Fland Dá Chongal of the Uí Failgi, and Éládach grandson of Máel Odar, of the Osraige, with many others.

Meantime, among the southern Uí Néill matters had been comparatively quiet. In 737 there had occurred a clash between the descendants of Áed Sláine at *Lia Ailbe* in Meath, in which Conaing son of Amalgaid had defeated Cernach son of Cathal, and Cathal son of Áed was slain. These latter two were of the incipient dynasty of Fir Cúl, a sub-kingdom around Kells which emerges into the light in the third and fourth decades of the eighth century, and whose rulers were descended from Ailill (†634), son of Áed Sláine. Conaing was of the kingdom of north Brega, whose rulers were descended from Congal (†634), also a son of Áed Sláine. What advantage this brought either side is far from clear. The clash may have been occasioned by attempts at expansion by the north Brega rulers, who at this time were pressing heavily on the Cianachta, and had taken over sufficient of the latter's territory to take over also the title of king of Cianachta, leaving the original rulers the title of kings of Ard Cianachta. However that may be, the clash was repeated in 743 at *Druim Derg*, somewhere in Brega, much to the disadvantage of the Fir Cúl, who lost their king, Dúngal son of Flann, and one Fergus son of Oistech. Conaing son of Amalgaid having been strangled in the previous year, it was another of his line,

Indrechtach son of Dúngalach, who profited by the victory.

While the lesser Meath kingdoms were thus busied in brawling with one another, the king of Meath, Domnall son of Murchad was free to indulge more extensive ambitions. In 743 he struck boldly at Áed Allán in a battle at *Seredmag* near Kells; and his gamble was successful. Áed Allán himself fell in the battle, along with Cumascach son of Conchobor king of Airthir, Móenach son of Conlaech, king of Uí Cremthainn, and Muiredach son of Fergus Forcraid, king of Uí Tuirtre. Oddly, Domnall, although now king of Tara, re-entered religion in 744 (he had already done so in 740). Presumably he combined his secular position with the abbacy of some monastery (perhaps Clonard), in the fashion more familiar to the kings of Cashel; it is quite clear, however, that he remained an active ruler to his death, two decades later, although in the second decade of his reign the Cenél nEógain, and the northern Uí Néill generally, began to present some threat to him. In 756 he found it necessary to recruit the Laigin in his support against Niall Frossach son of Fergal, of the Cenél nEógain, although nothing decisive seems to have come of it one way or the other. He was still king of Tara at his death on 20 November 763; but he was succeeded immediately and without apparent difficulty by Niall Frossach. It may be assumed that the sons of Domnall were in no position to contest the succession, the more so as two years later, in 765, two of them pushed their disagreements so far as to fight a pitched battle at Carn in Westmeath. The loser was Murchad, the winner Donnchad, who had the support of Follaman son of Cú Chongalt, king of Meath. Follaman was himself treacherously killed in the following year, presumably by or at the instigation of Donnchad, who as a result assumed the kingship of the southern Uí Néill. Connected with this change, no doubt, was the fighting in this same year between the men of Meath and of

Brega, in which two notables, Máeluma son of Tuathal and Donngal son of Doreith were slain.

The Laigin 738–778

Among the Laigin, the battle of *Áth Senaig* ended the *de facto* dominance that Áed Mend son of Colcu had enjoyed. Later texts give his pre-eminence no recognition, and assume that on the death of Fáelán in 738 the rule of the Laigin passed uninterruptedly to Bran Bec son of Murchad, who fell in the same battle. Into his place stepped his brother Muiredach, who enjoyed two decades of comparative peace, as did the Uí Ceinnselaigh in the south, and the Uí Failgi on the west.

The buffer state of the Osraige, to the west of the Uí Ceinnselaigh, was less placid. Its rulers in the early part of the century were of slight importance. Cellach son of Fáelchar had been killed in battle between the Laigin and the men of Munster in 735; his successor, Forbasach son of Ailill, was of no significance, and was slain in 740. The next ruler of the Osraige proved rather more aggressive than his predecessors: Anmchaid, son of Cú Cerca, two years after his accession, devastated the Delbna and Cenél Fiachach, in the stretch of country between the Uí Failgi and the Shannon, and in 745 inflicted a defeat on the Déisi, under Uargus son of Fiachra Enboth, at *Ard Meic Uidhir*. In

Fig. 21.

THE UÍ FAILGI IN THE EIGHTH CENTURY

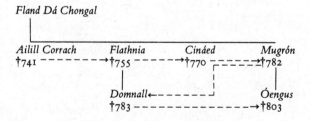

Fland Dá Chongal

| Ailill Corrach | Flathnia | Cináed | Mugrón |
| †741 | †755 | †770 | †782 |

Domnall †783

Óengus †803

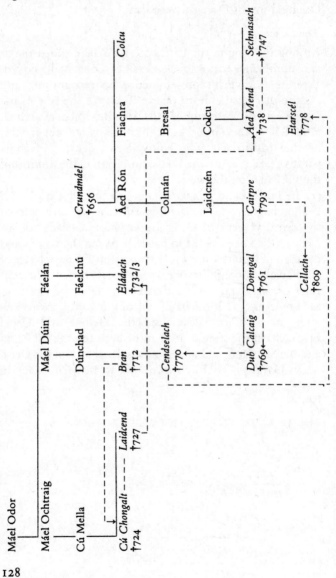

Fig. 22.

RULERS OF THE UÍ CEINNSELAIGH IN THE EIGHTH CENTURY

128

Cathal grandson of Cináed (†758) is unaccounted for.

Fig. 23.

RULERS OF THE OSRAIGE 693–802

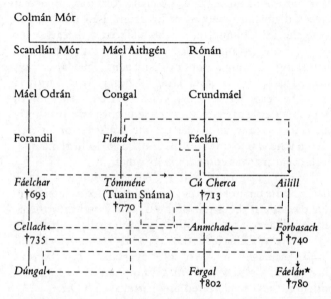

*Fáelán's successor, Máel Dúin son of Cummascach, is otherwise unidentified.

the following year, 747, he inflicted a defeat on three sons of one Cumscrach, whose contemporary notoriety is as undoubted as their identity is now obscure. Three years later, he was to be found engaging in a clash at *Inis Snaic*, and in 754 he devastated the Fothairt. Five years later, he was engaged in battle with the Laigin, apparently with results satisfactory to himself. The end of his reign is obscure, and his successor, Tómméne son of Flann, enjoys an equal obscurity up to his death by violence in 770. The Osraige for some time past had been enjoying internal disputes over the succession, and one such battle for internal supremacy took place in 769, in which Tómméne defeated the sons of Cellach son of Fáelchar.

Muiredach's successor as king of the Laigin, Cellach, son of his brother Dúnchad, was equally fortunate (one year excepted) in the quietness of his reign. Less undisturbed were the Uí Ceinnselaigh, who suffered a defeat at the hands of the Osraige at Gowran in 761, with the loss of their king, Donngal son of Laidcnén. The latter was succeeded by his brother Dub Calgcaig, who survived for eight years before being killed by Cennselach son of Bran in a battle at Ferns in 769. He in turn was promptly killed in the following year by one Etarscél, son of Áed Mend, who was to rule until his death in 778. The remainder of the century was comparatively quiet.

The sole exceptional year in Cellach's reign was 770. In that year the territory of the Laigin suffered some considerable damage at the hands of the Uí Néill, and they themselves inflicted some on south Brega. Internally, a challenge was offered to Cellach's authority, oddly enough, by the Uí Failgi, primarily by two sons of Flann Dá Chongal, Cináed and Cellach, and one Cathnia son of Bécc, of the Fothairt; these he defeated in a battle at *Áth Orc*.

The kingship of Cashel 742–792

West of the Laigin, in the kingdom of Cashel, the dominating personality of Cathal son of Finnguine had passed from the scene in 742; and at his death there comes a break. He may have been succeeded by one Cathasach, son or nephew of Etarscél, a previous king of Cashel; but if so, nothing is known of him.

All these were drawn from the Eóganacht of east Munster. The kingship then passed, at least nominally, to the king of the Eóganacht of Loch Léin, Máel Dúin son of Áed, whose rule, such as it was, lasted until his death in 786. That Munster, or a large part of it, was seen by outsiders to be peculiarly vulnerable at this time is suggested by the

Fig. 24.

RULERS OF WEST MUNSTER IN THE SEVENTH AND
EIGHTH CENTURIES
(Eóganacht of Loch Léin)

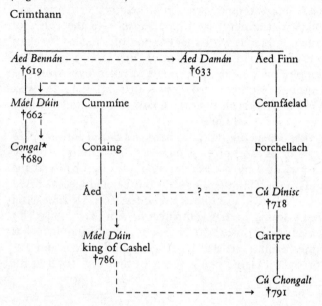

*Apparently succeeded by one Máel Mracho, of whose background
nothing is known.

activities of Donnchad, king of Tara: in 775, after an
encounter between the men of Munster and the Uí Néill,
the latter did great devastation in Munster. This was
followed in 776 by a battle between them in which the
community of Durrow were involved, and in which the
Munstermen suffered heavy losses.

In repelling attacks from without, Máel Dúin laboured
under the disadvantage of not enjoying wholehearted
support from his own subordinates. The rising kingdom of
the Ciarraige was uneasy in its subordination to the

Eóganacht of Loch Léin, and would have preferred to be subordinate to the king of Cashel, who had the advantage of being further away; and their unease communicated itself to other subordinate kingdoms. The accession of Máel Dúin was used, either in his reign or soon after, as a device to transfer Ciarraige allegiance to the rulers of Cashel, bolstered with a fake synod of saints of the sixth century, in which Brendan of Birr and Brendan of Clonfert (whom the Ciarraige had taken over from the vanishing Altraige) prophesied that no king of west Munster would rule over the Ciarraige from the days of a king named Máel Dúin.

After Mael Dúin's death, there was gross confusion. His successor as king of west Munster, Cú Chongelt son of Cairpre, died by violence in 791, not improbably at the hands of the Ciarraige, as did his brother and successor Áed in 803. In the kingship of Cashel, for six years after Mael Dúin's death, there was in effect no Eóganacht ruler: his immediate successor was Ólchobor son of Flann, who was of the Érainn people of Uí Fidgenti in the west, and was moreover a cleric, being abbot of Scattery Island at his

Fig. 25.

UÍ FIDGENTI IN THE EIGHTH CENTURY

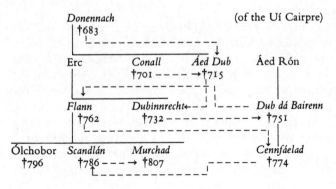

132

death in 796. Exactly what his standing was as king of Cashel, whether acting or figurehead, is not the least obscure question in the whole episode: the utmost that can be extracted from the scanty evidence is that the Eóganacht at the time were rent by internal strife, probably between east and west, which took some years to sort out.

Finally, in 792, a candidate either sufficiently acceptable or sufficiently forceful emerges, one Artrí son of Cathal of the Eóganacht of Glennamain. He succeeded to the kingship of Cashel in 792, and of his accession the term *ordinatio* is used, which seems to imply some kind of ecclesiastical intervention in his elevation. His position was sufficiently solid to last until his death in 821.

Connacht 742–803

In Connacht, as usual, matters are a little clearer. Áed Balb, who died in 742, and his two predecessors, seem to have preferred a quiet life; and they seem to have aroused no active opposition. Shortly after the death of Áed Balb, when the kingship of Connacht had passed to another son of Cellach, named Fergus, trouble broke out. In the south of Connacht the Uí Maine and the Uí Fiachrach of Aidne fell to fighting in 743, and in the north, in Moylurg, the Uí Ailella and the Gailenga did likewise. In neither case is a decisive result reported, and the reason for the clashes is unknown. There is some likelihood that Fergus may not have been a particularly strong ruler, possibly due to divisions within the Uí Briúin. In 746 he was involved, on the losing side, with the Conmaicne, in a battle whose protagonists, while difficult to identify with certainty, very probably belonged to the Uí Briúin; but in the same year he was successful in inflicting a slaughter on the southern Uí Briúin, the Uí Briúin Seola. This seems to have eliminated or discouraged whatever internal opposition there was to him, and it became possible to turn his undivided attention elsewhere. In 752 he crushed the Calraige of Moylurg to

Fig. 26.

CENÉL CAIRPRE IN THE SEVENTH AND EIGHTH CENTURIES

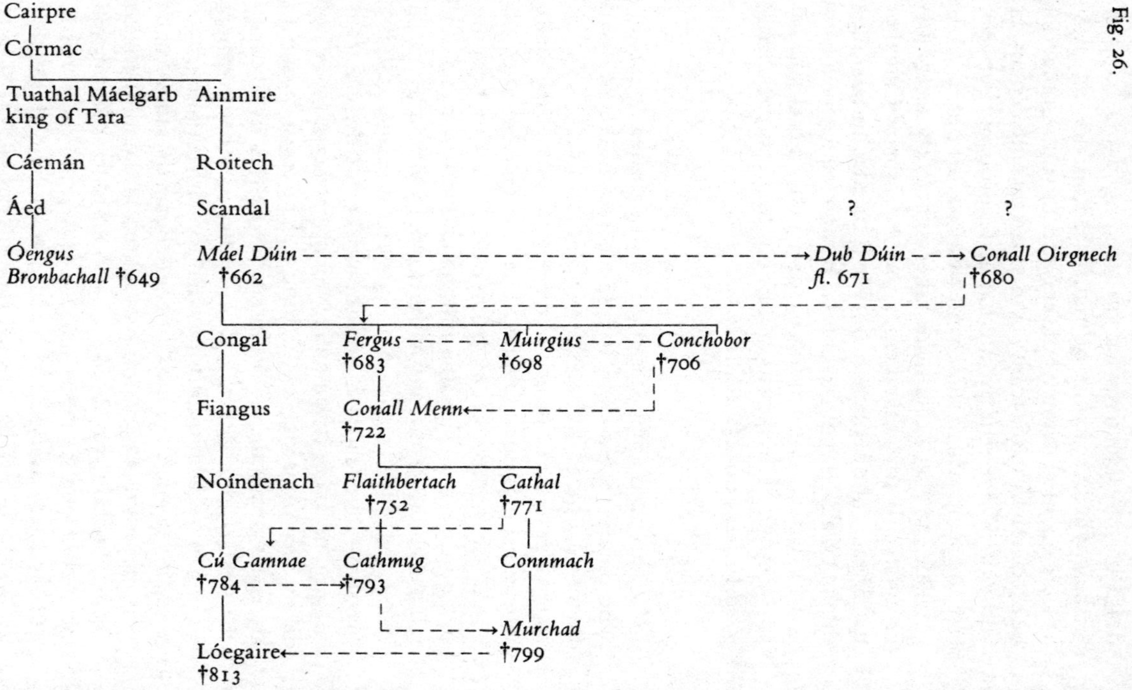

Cairpre
|
Cormac
|
Tuathal Máelgarb
king of Tara

Cáemán
|
Áed
|
Óengus
Bronbachall †649

Ainmire
|
Roitech
|
Scandal
|
Máel Dúin
†662

→ Dub Dúin - - → Conall Oirgnech
fl. 671   †680
?   ?

Congal — Fergus — Muirgius — Conchobor
          †683   †698   †706

Fiangus — Conall Menn
           †722

Noíndenach — Flaithbertach — Cathal
              †752   †771

Cú Gamnae — Cathmug — Commach
†784   †793

Lóegaire — - → Murchad
†813   †799

the north. In 754 he turned on the Cenél Cairpre, and fought a battle with them at Ardneeskin, of which, despite a heavy loss of life, no decisive result is reported. The attack was renewed in 756 at *Móin Mór* (perhaps in Longford), where the Cenél Cairpre were decisively defeated. By the mid-century they were in any case split in two by the expanding kingdom of Uí Briúin of Bréifne.

Fergus died on pilgrimage in that same year, and the kingship of Connacht was seized by Ailill Medraige, son of the Indrechtach killed in 707. That this was resented by the Uí Briúin is beyond doubt, and he was challenged by them at Breaffy in 758. The Uí Briúin lost heavily; their casualties included three grandsons of Cellach, by name Cathmug, Cathrannach and Artbran, all possible contenders for the kingship. As usual, however, the effects were no more than temporary. Elsewhere, the Cenél Cairpre had more than recovered from their defeat at *Móin Mór*, and in 762 defeated the Luigne at Kiltabeg in Longford; while in 764 Ailill himself died, of wounds according to report, though it is not clear by whom they were inflicted, or when – possibly in the slaughter of the Connachta at *Cuilnech Mór* in 763, in which the slaughterers are unidentified.

Ailill was replaced by Dubinnrecht of the Uí Briúin, son of the Cathal who had died in 635. It might be expected that he would be opposed by the Uí Fiachrach, but if so, there is no evidence that it came to the stage of battle. Instead, he found himself in conflict with the Conmaicne at Shrule in Longford in 766, where he inflicted a defeat on them and what seem to have been their allies from among the Luigne, of whom Áed Dub son of Taichlech was the most prominent casualty.

On the death of Dubinnrecht, apparently from dysentery, in 768, the Uí Fiachrach made a brief come-back in the person of Donn Chothaid, son of Ailill Medraige. His rule was uneventful, and on his death in 773 the kingship of Connacht reverted to the Uí Briúin, under Flaithrí, a son of the Domnall who died in 728. His rule is marked by a recrudescence of restlessness on the part of the Uí Maine, who clashed with, and were defeated by, Flaithrí at *Achad Liag* in Roscommon in 775. On his death in 777, a year marked by fresh activity on the part of the Uí Fiachrach, with a slaughter of the Calraige, the rule of Connacht passed, peacefully it seems, to Artgal, brother of the late Dubinnrecht. He also had his problems with the Uí Maine, whom he defeated with some slaughter in *Mag Dairben*, beside L. Ree in Galway, in 778; but active kingship seems not to have been greatly to his taste, for in 782/3 he departed on pilgrimage to Iona, where he died in 791. His absence left behind a state of confusion in which the most prominent and active candidate for the kingship was Tipraite son of Tadc, apparently of the Uí Briúin. In 784 he inflicted a defeat on the Uí Fiachrach of Aidne at Bally-connell, and in the following year gained a victory on the Moy, presumably against the Uí Fiachrach of the north. Any prospect of this being followed up was cut short by Tipraite's death in 786. Confusion continued: in 787 the Uí Briúin suffered a defeat at the hands of the Uí Fiachrach at Gola, and in the same year they inflicted a slaughter on the Uí Briúin of the Owles, in which all the latter's notables were wiped out, including their king, Flaithgal son of Flannabra. After a year's breathing space, conflict again flared up in the battle of *Druim Góise*, in which the loser was a section of the Uí Briúin under Fogartach, son of the Cathal who died in 735; who the winners were is unclear, most probably the branch of the Uí Briúin led by Muirgius son of Tomaltach. Elsewhere the Uí Ailella were attempting to expand their territory at the expense of the Luigne, on whom they inflicted a slaughter at *Achad Abla* in Sligo and followed this up in 790 with a battle at Agharois in Sligo in which they defeated the Luigne decisively. The political background to this is complicated further by the fact that there is some reason to suppose that the Uí Ailella were supporting that section of the Uí Briúin led by Muirgius son of Tomaltach, and that the Luigne were supporting his opponents. Which had precedence, conflict between the Uí Ailella and the Luigne as such, or their support of diverse Uí Briúin factions, is impossible to say.

The tension between the factions within the Uí Briúin in 792 resolved itself in a set battle at *Sruithe Cluana Argaid* in which Muirgius defeated and killed Cinaed son of Artgal; it was followed by another at *Ard Maic Rime* which effectively overthrew the Uí Ailella, and eliminated from the scene Conchobor and Airechtach, two grandsons of Cathal, Cathmuǵ son of Flaithbertach, king of Cairpre, and Cormac son of Dub dá Crích, king of Bréifne. Neither battle, bloody though they were, settled matters finally: four years later, in 796, Muirgius suffered a defeat at *Áth Féne* in Mayo, but within three years had sufficiently recovered to be able to defeat his opponents at *Dún Ganiba*. Within three years again he had asserted his overlordship over the subordinate kingdoms of Connacht by destroying the chief stronghold of the Uí Maine at Loch Ree. Thenceforth, he was effectively master of Connacht until his death in 815.

Ulidia 735–801

The affairs of the Ulaid, after the death of Áed Rón in battle in 735, impinge very little on the rest of the country. His successor was of the Dál nAraide, one Cathasach, a nephew of the late Cú Chuaráin; and the latter seems, on obtaining the kingship of Ulidia, to have relinquished the kingship of Dál nAraide in favour of Indrechtach, son of the Lethlobar slain in 709. As king of Ulidia, he survived for some fourteen years, when he was slain at Rathveagh in Antrim, probably in the interest of the Dál Fiatach, to whom the kingship passed. The new ruler, Bresal, son of Áed Rón, was promptly killed in 750, without however losing the Dál Fiatach the kingship, which passed to Bresal's brother

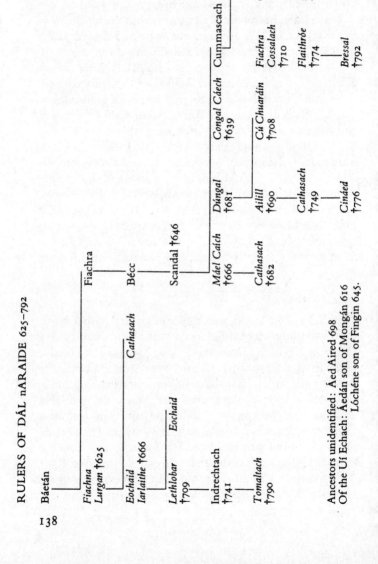

Fig. 27.

RULERS OF DÁL nARAIDE 625–792

138

Báetán
Fiachra Lurgan †625 — Fiachra
Eochaid Iarlaithe †666 — Cathasach
Léthlobar †709 — Eochaid — Eochaid
Indrechtach †741
Tomaltach †790
Bécc
Scandal †646
Máel Cáich †666 — Dúngal †681 — Congal Cáech †639 — Cummascach — Congalach
Cathasach †682
Ailill †690 — Cú Chuarán †708
Cathasach †749
Cinéed †776
Fiachra Cossalach †710
Flaithróe †774 — Dub dá Inber †727
Bressal †792

Ancestors unidentified: Áed Aired 698
Of the Uí Echach: Áedán son of Mongán 616
Lóchéne son of Fingin 645.

Fiachna. This latter was to rule Ulidia for almost four decades.

Some of the stresses visible in the 730s still persisted during his reign. Tension between the Ulaid and the Uí Néill, intermittently focussed on Armagh, flickered up again in 759 in the battle of Emain, occasioned by a conflict between Airechtach, priest of Armagh, and Fer dá Crích, the abbot thereof: a battle which Fiachna won, though to what benefit to himself is unclear. To his north, he clashed with, and defeated, the Uí Echach of Cuib at *Áth Dumai* in Down in 761; the latters' king, Ailill son of Feidlimid, was one of the casualties. The Dál nAraide, however, were on the whole too divided to make a plausible bid to oust Fiachna. In 776 they lost one of their magnates, Nia son of Cú Allaid, in an internecine battle at Slemish, and in the same year indulged in the luxury of another battle at *Drong*, in which Cinaed of Carraig, king of Dál nAraide, and his supporter Dúngal, grandson of Fergus Forcraid and king of the Uí Tuirtri, fell to Tomaltach son of Indrechtach and his backer, Eochaid son of Fiachna. The same year witnessed yet another battle at *Áth Dumai* between the Uí Echach of Cuib and the Airthir, in which the former lost their king, Gormgal son of Conall Crú. Seven years later, in 783, the conflicts within the Dál nAraide broke into the open once more in a battle at Dunaughey in Antrim, in which the most prominent casualty was Fócarta, another grandson of Cú Allaid.

In the circumstances, Fiachna seemed to be well settled in the kingship of Ulidia: which may have had some connection with the mysterious meeting with Donnchad, king of Tara, at *Inis na Ríg* in eastern Brega in 784. The latter may have intended to propose some kind of treaty delimiting their respective spheres of influence; it seems not improbable that Donnchad was at the time involving himself in the affairs of the Airthir, and perhaps also with the Uí Echach, who in 786 were to fight a battle at *Cenu* (perhaps in Louth) with the Conaille in which the Mugdorna were involved, with the loss of their king Cathróe. Some considerable caution on Fiachna's part is suggested by his recorded reluctance to step on the same shore as Donnchad (he apparently remained in a boat off-shore), and there is no record, explicit or implicit, of any positive outcome to the meeting.

Fiachna died in 789. For a brief period the overlordship of Ulidia was seized and held by Tomaltach son of Indrechtach of the Dál nAraide; he was dispossessed in battle in the same year, and he himself slain, by Eochaid, son of the late Fiachna. In the following year the Dál nAraide countered by inflicting a slaughter on the Dál Fiatach, without however shaking Eochaid's position; and in 801 he restored the balance of honours by defeating and slaying in battle Eochu son of Ailill, king of the Uí Echach.

The Uí Néill 766–805

From 766, although the kingship of Tara was held by Niall Frossach, the predominant figure among the Uí Néill was Donnchad son of Domnall, king of Uisnech. In 770 he clashed with the Laigin under Cellach son of Dúnchad: the aggression was initiated by Donnchad, who brought his army as far south as Skenagun in Kildare, with the Laigin prudently avoiding battle; then, abandoning the attempt to induce them to stand and face him, he camped for a week at Knockaulin, and harried and burned the territory of the Laigin. Having thus demonstrated his capacities on an extern territory, he made a hosting to the north, and in 772 yet another hosting to *Cnoc Báine* in Tyrone; of neither is any clear result recorded, but they presumably served to overawe the northern Uí Néill. Niall Frossach, of advanced years, was not disposed to oppose him. In 774, Donnchad caused a disturbance at the *óenach* of Teltown, very probably a calculated provocation. For all practical purposes, from 772 he was king of Tara in all but name.

Fig. 28.

THE SUB-DYNASTIES OF BREGA

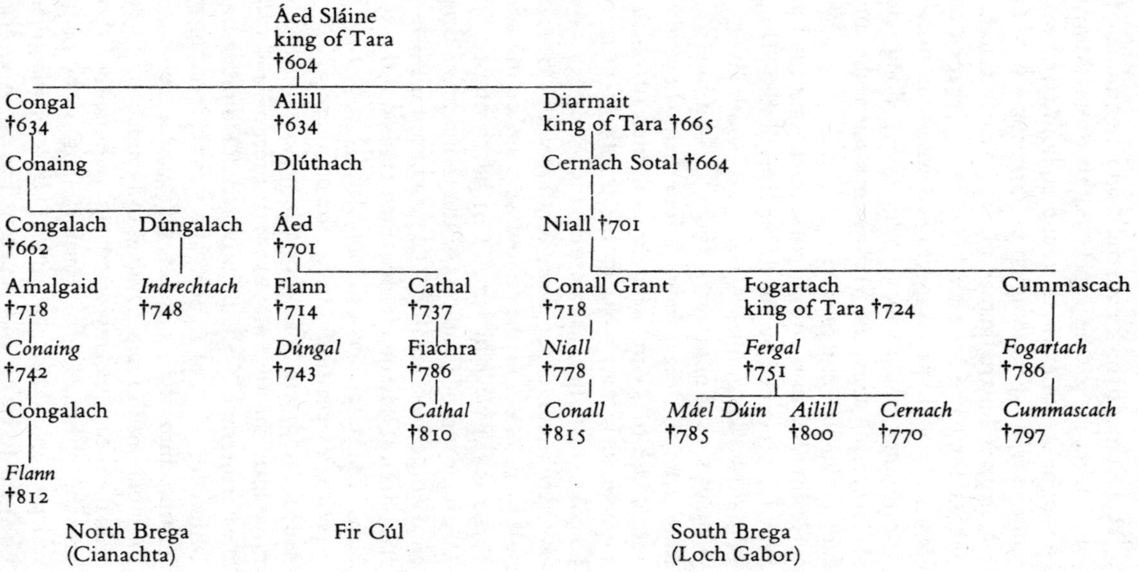

		Áed Sláine king of Tara †604					
Congal †634		Ailill †634		Diarmait king of Tara †665			
Conaing		Dlúthach		Cernach Sotal †664			
Congalach †662	Dúngalach	Áed †701		Niall †701			
Amalgaid †718	*Indrechtach* †748	Flann †714	Cathal †737	Conall Grant †718	Fogartach king of Tara †724		Cummascach
Conaing †742		*Dúngal* †743	Fiachra †786	*Niall* †778	*Fergal* †751		*Fogartach* †786
Congalach			*Cathal* †810	*Conall* †815	*Máel Dúin* †785	*Ailill* *Cernach* †800 †770	*Cummascach* †797
Flann †812							

141
    North Brega   Fir Cúl   South Brega
    (Cianachta)   (Loch Gabor)

Reluctance to pick a quarrel cannot be numbered among his defects. In 775 he struck southwards at Munster, and wrought great devastation; and on home territory, in the same year, he was indulging in skirmishing with the community of Clonard. In the following year he fought a battle with the men of Munster (who were perhaps attempting reprisals for the previous year's devastation) in which the community of Durrow were involved, along with some of Domnall's sons; the Munstermen suffered heavy losses, and Donnchad emerged victor.

Within his own lordship of Uisnech, his chief problem was that presented by the descendants of Áed Sláine, rulers of the two kingdoms of north and south Brega. In 777 there was spasmodic warfare between him and Congalach, king of north Brega, and he is reported to have 'disturbed' the óenach of Teltown against the men of north Brega. Donnchad in fact went to the length of recruiting the Laigin in his support against the men of Brega, with what concrete results is not clear. Warfare with Congalach was still in progress in the following year, culminating in a battle at *Forcaladh* in which Congalach himself fell, with Diarmait son of Clothgna of the Cianacht of Brega, and many others less notable. The men of south Brega seem to have been at least quiescent in these clashes, and may indeed have been supporters of Donnchad.

With his position among the southern Uí Néill thus consolidated, and Niall Frossach, nominally king of Tara, now dead, the next move was to assert his authority over the northern Uí Néill, in the person of Domnall son of Áed Muinderg, king of Ailech. This was achieved in 779 by a hosting into the north of sufficient force to overawe Domnall into giving hostages to Donnchad.

In the meantime, his former allies among the Laigin were proving restless. In 780, Ruaidrí, king of the Laigin, and Cairpre son of Laidcnén, king of Uí Ceinnselaigh, invaded Uí Néill territory and penetrated as far as *Óchtar Ochae* near Kells, where they were blocked by Donnchad and driven southwards, with Donnchad in pursuit, ravaging their territory and churches. On a lesser scale, in the following year, the men of Cualu seem to have made a foray over the Rye into Brega, and were defeated on All Hallows day by the men of Brega, for once united: the north under two nephews of the late Congalach, Diarmait and Conaing, the south under Máel Dúin son of Fergus and Fógartach son of Cumascach.

Unity of this kind presented an obvious threat to Donnchad, and in 784 he held a meeting (already mentioned) with Áed Rón, king of Ulidia, at *Inis na Ríg* in eastern Brega, perhaps to make a treaty of non-aggression. The meeting seems to have had no very substantial results. At the same time, in the north, Domnall son of Áed enhanced his standing by a victory over the Cenél mBógaine. In 786, then, Donnchad dealt with the descendants of Áed Sláine in a battle at Leafin in Meath: in it fell Fiachra son of Cathal, king of Fir Cúl, Fócartach son of Cumascach, king of south Brega, and Conaing and Diarmait, the two leaders of north Brega.

A year later, the position among the northern Uí Néill took a more satisfactory turn for Donnchad with the defeat of Domnall son of Áed in battle by Máel Dúin son of Áed Allán of the Cenél nEógain; Domnall escaped by flight. Two years later, the defeat was repeated at the river Clady in Donegal by Áed Oirdnide, a son of Niall Frossach, and once again Domnall escaped by flight.

In his turn, Áed Oirdnide was beginning to present a threat, and a more imminent one than Domnall son of Áed had done. By 791 matters had come to a head in a battle at Teltown in which Donnchad defeated Áed 'the undutiful', as he was nicknamed, and in which Cathal son of Eochaid, king of Uí Crimthainn, Máel Fothartaig son of Artrí of Fernmag, and one Domnall son of Colcu, backers of Áed Oirdnide, were slain; Áed himself survived to fight another day, a day which was some time in coming. By 794 Donnchad felt sufficiently secure to take a hosting in support of the Laigin against the men of Munster, and Áed profited thereby to invade Mugdorna Maigen, not, it seems, with any very solid result.

His opportunity came three years later, in the battle of Drumree in Meath, in which Donnchad was defeated and killed, with his brother Diarmait Odar, and many others. Áed signalised the beginning of his rule as king of Tara by devastating Meath, and thereafter abandoned the area largely to its own devices, which were for the most part violent and focussed on the kingship of Uisnech. In a battle at Fennor in Tethba, in 799, Murchadh son of Domnall, who is otherwise unidentified, but presumably a brother of the late Donnchad, defeated a coalition of Fergus son of Algal, Coscrach son of Ceithernach, who apparently were of the ruling line, and two kings of Cenél Cairpre, Dubinnrecht son of Artgal and Murchad son of Connmach. He may have been acting in the interests of Donnchad's son Domnall, but in that same year the latter was slain in treachery by·his own kinsmen, probably by his brothers Conchobor and Ailill, who continued to dispute the kingship of Meath. In 802 Áed Oirdnide, determined to put an end to this quarrelling, raised a hosting against Meath and attempted to settle the matter by the classically ineffectual expedient of dividing Meath between them. The division lasted a year, at the most: in 803, Conchobor defeated Ailill and slew him in the battle of Rathconnell in Westmeath, and thenceforth ruled as undisturbedly as a king could expect, though with one eye on the kingship of Tara.

This was unlikely to be vacant for some time, for Áed was proving himself a vigorous and adroit man of war. In 804 he devastated the territory of the Laigin twice within a month, and later in the year made a hosting against them and obtained the submission of Fínnechta, king of the Laigin. In the following year, being for some reason dissatisfied with this arrangement, he made a hosting to *Dún Cuair*, and undeterred by his experience in Meath, divided the territory of the Laigin between Muiredach son of Ruaidrí and Muiredach son of Bran. The arrangement proved equally ephemeral: within a very short time Fínnechta defeated Muiredach son of Ruaidrí twice, and resumed his former position as king of the Laigin.

The church after the great plague

The church in the late seventh century has changed little from the early part of the century. The great monastic confederations dominate the scene, and the principal cause of dispute is still the question of the date of Easter. This had of course been in progress since well before the great plague: a mission of enquiry had been sent to Rome in 631, to study the Roman method of computing the date of Easter, and had reported on its return against the Irish method of computation as being out of step with that of the rest of Christendom. The argument goes back to the beginning of the century, as does the accompanying interest in the computus, or body of rules for making such computations: Sillán, abbot of Bangor who died in 610, is credited with having introduced into Ireland the Easter cycle of Dionisius Exiguus. By the late 630s most of the monasteries in the south of the country had switched over to the Roman method of computation, and it has been suggested that one reason the northern monasteries found the presence of Mochuda at Rahen in Uí Néill territory so distasteful was that he practised the Roman method, rather than the older Irish method which they themselves preferred. The change to the Roman method throughout the country was accomplished slowly; Armagh seems to have been foremost in its adoption in the north, while the federation of monasteries subject to Iona seem to have been the last to accept it, yielding only in 716.

The dispute is itself not particularly important, but

among its by-products was a more eager pursuit of learn-ing: not only computistic learning, but also the study of the fathers of the Church, in search of support for one or the other position in the dispute. The staple intellectual diet of the monasteries was still, as it had always been, the Old and New Testaments; but these needed to be approached, not only directly, but also with the aid of Jerome and Augustine; to comprehend the sacred text, it was necessary to study Latin grammar, and be able to construe the unfamiliar structure of the Latin sentence. In addition to this, since much of the Old Testament was history, this also should be studied. The book of books was 'an encyclopaedia which contained all knowledge useful to man, both sacred and profane ... The student needs language, grammar and history in order to understand the literal sense, dialectic to distinguish true doctrine from false, arithmetic for number symbolism, natural history for the symbolism of beasts and birds ...' – save that Irish churchmen as a rule by-passed these last elaborations and stuck as closely as possible to the literal sense of Scripture, which made quite sufficient demands on their capacities and libraries. Of classical learning, leaving aside scraps and fragments of Greek and mangled Hebrew, and leaving aside also the rather doubtful case of Columbanus of Bobbio, there is no certain example in this period: passages which seem to reflect the classics may rather derive either from the grammarians, such as Donatus and Priscian, who used classical quotations freely to exemplify rules, or from such fathers of the Church as Jerome, who was steeped in the classics. Law also derived primarily from the Bible, but to it were added both the decisions of continental and African synods, and the decisions of Irish synods: all this brought together early in the eighth century in a collection of canons which is associated with the scribe Rúbín (†725) of Dairinis on the Blackwater, and Cú Cuimne (†747) of Iona.

Before the great plague, celibacy had been the rule for

ecclesiastics. By the time of Rúbín and Cú Cuimne, it has come to be assumed that an abbot, for example, need not be in orders, and by the middle of the eighth century hereditary succession to abbacies is to be found in a number

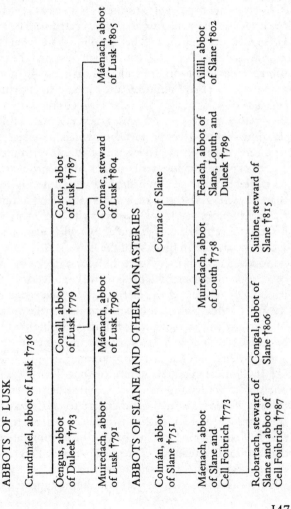

Fig. 29.

ABBOTS OF LUSK

Crundmáel, abbot of Lusk †736

Óengus, abbot of Duleek †783 — Conall, abbot of Lusk †779 — Colcu, abbot of Lusk †787

Muiredach, abbot of Lusk †791 — Máenach, abbot of Lusk †796 — Cormac, steward of Lusk †804 — Máenach, abbot of Lusk †805

ABBOTS OF SLANE AND OTHER MONASTERIES

Colmán, abbot of Slane †751

Cormac of Slane

Máenach, abbot of Slane and Cell Foibrich †773 — Muiredach, abbot of Louth †758 — Fedach, abbot of Slane, Louth, and Duleek †789 — Ailill, abbot of Slane †802

Robartach, steward of Slane and abbot of Cell Foibrich †787 — Congal, abbot of Slane †806 — Suibne, steward of Slane †815 of monasteries (see Fig. 29). It is matter for remark in his obit in 806 that Congal son of Máenach, abbot of Slane, died a virgin. This development is in effect a closer integration than before of the church into Irish society and of Irish society into the church.

Yet another type of integration is visible in the extension of ecclesiastical protection to various categories of persons in the eighth century. The headline had been set by Adomnán, abbot of Iona, who in 697 obtained the consent of the chief rulers in Ireland to Iona's taking under its protection women, children and clerics. Such protection (*snádud*) was of course a familiar legal concept at the time, in a rather more limited sense: any person of full legal standing could give protection, which in effect means immunity from legal process, for a period of time and an extent of place varying with the rank of the 'protector', and provided that the person protected was of no higher rank than himself; and to slay or wound such a person rendered the guilty party liable for a payment to the 'protector' of his full honour-price, over and above what was due to the victim or his kin. In the case of the 'Law of Adomnán', this is modified to a payment of the honour-price of the victim, or a proportion thereof. The 'law' was renewed in 727, but in so far as it affected the clergy it was superseded by the 'Law of Patrick', which took all clerics under the protection of Armagh, in 734. Both were followed during the century by a rash of other such 'laws', of obscure content, promulgated by such monasteries as Clonmacnois (744), Rahen (743), Clonfert (744), Roscommon (772), Emly (784), and one placed under the name of Columcille in 753. Of all these it should be noted that they had to be renewed quite frequently, by agreement with the ruler of a given territory: the 'law' of Ciarán (of Clonmacnois), promulgated with the 'law' of Brendan (of Clonfert) in 744 by Fergus son of Cellach, king of Connacht, was renewed in 788; that of Rahen was renewed, five years after it first appeared in 743, but applied only to the northern half of the country. The 'law' of Patrick was promulgated in Connacht in 783 by Dub dá Leithi, successor of Patrick, and Tipraite son of Tadc, king of Connacht, in concert, and again by Gormgal son of Díndatach, successor of Patrick, in 798; the 'law' of Ailbe, promulgated in 793, applied only to Munster.

Indeed, a particularly striking phenomenon of the second half of the seventh century and of the eighth is the emergence of Armagh from comparative obscurity to a position in which it could challenge and outstrip Iona and Clonmacnois in its claims to ecclesiastical lordship. Its basic lordship covered an area roughly equivalent to the kingdom of Airthir, with adjoining portions of the kingdoms of the Dál Fiatach and Dál nAraide. By about 700, however, it was claiming suzerainty over churches scattered much more widely: all churches free from secular burdens, all churches yet unattached to any of the great monastic foundations, all churches whose names contained the element *domnach* – a very early borrowing of Latin *dominica*. Tírechán, writing between 670 and 700, specified many such churches in the territories of the Uí Néill, north and south, and in Connacht, adding however that some had been pilfered from Armagh by Iona or encroached on by Clonmacnois since the great plague of 664–6; other properties in the southern half of the country are specified elsewhere, although Armagh seems to have accepted Kildare's claims to a great part of Laigin territory as its *paruchia*. Within the canonical sphere also, Armagh claimed to be subject only to the see of Rome, and to be superior to all other ecclesiastical authorities in Ireland. In effect, it was claiming an 'over-kingship' within the Irish church. These claims seem to have met with a measure of acceptance: Áed, bishop of Sletty in Carlow, formally accepted Ségéne (†688), bishop of Armagh, as his overlord; and his successor Conchad accepted Ségéne's successor, Flann Febla (†715).

Another phenomenon of the late eighth-century church was the custom of taking relics on circuit. This habit crops up first in connection with the smallpox epidemic of 742–3, when the relics of Trian, of Kildalkey in Meath, were so taken round, presumably with prophylactic intentions. The second half of the century was to provide ample scope for such a deployment of relics. In 773 there was unusual drought and a consequent famine, and the following year saw an epidemic of dysentery, which was repeated in 777 and 778; in 778–9 there was a widespread murrain of cattle, and this was accompanied in 779 by famine and smallpox. Four years later there was an epidemic of influenzal pneumonia, and again in 786. During these years of death and disaster occur a number of examples of relics going on circuit: in 776 Slane and Clonard brought round the relics of their founders, Erc and Finnian, as did Ardbraccan in 785 with the relics of Ultán. Similarly with the relics of Coemgin of Glendalough and Mochua of Clondalkin in 790, those of Tole of Clonard in 793, and those, again, of Trian of Kildalkey in 794. It seems probable that other monasteries elsewhere in the country did likewise: the Meath bias of these examples is due to the annals which supply this information having drawn from a set of annals compiled probably at Clonard from the middle of the century onwards. The relics as they made their circuit were the object of offerings to the monastery which possessed them, and this in time hardened into custom, to become a lucrative source of income to their fortunate possessors.

It is likely, however, that the population of the monasteries themselves had in some degree been thinned out by the recurrent epidemics, reducing the number of suitable candidates for office; for it is from the 770s onwards that the holding of a plurality of abbacies or offices becomes noticeable. Do-Dimóc, who died in 748, was abbot both of Clonard and Kildare; Senchán, who died in 796, was abbot both of Killeigh and of Birr; and examples are not uncommon. This was one possible reaction to the disasters of those decades; another, not necessarily exclusive of the first, was to see in them the vengeance of God for sin. This is rarely seen on any large scale: an exception is the case in 772, on the feast of Michael, which was marked by thunder and lightning, 'like the day of judgment', and which provoked terror intense enough to cause people to fast for two three-day periods, with only one meal between. Within the church itself, there appears a movement of ascetic revival, looking back for its exemplars to Columcille and Comgall and Finnian of Clonard. The most eminent of these was Máel Ruain of Tallaght, who died in 792, and was in contact with a number of others of similar views, the majority of whom seem to have been in the south of the country. In some respects their views are parallel to those of the Christians in Ireland before the mid-sixth century: Máel Ruain told his disciple Máel Díthruib not to meddle with worldly disputes, to go with no man to law or to an assembly on any man's account, but to stay in his church, to pray and to instruct those who came for instruction. Compromise was ruled out, either in principle or practice.

The ascetic reform had however no machinery for renewing itself. Each church attached to the reform during Mael Rúain's lifetime was dependent on the character of its abbot to maintain its level of asceticism; a new abbot could overturn it well-nigh overnight. No authority existed to maintain a check on any individual monastery, to prevent it slipping away from its standards. The ascetic reform had indeed a future, but not an institutional one: it survived rather as an inspiration to small groups of ascetics and individuals.

* * *

By the end of the eighth century, this society, both secular and ecclesiastical, had come to a state of comparative stability. The ruling dynasties in the various provinces were still expanding and provoking conflict, still shedding branches incapable of grasping power, and this process was to continue; in the church, the ascetic reform was able to keep the ecclesiastical body from becoming too flabby, intermeshed though it was with the world. Stability of this kind, however, could continue only as long as no new ingredient was injected to upset the balance, which might otherwise be self-righting. That ingredient appeared first in 798, when the Norsemen burnt Inis Patraic, and broke the shrine of Do-Chonna, and committed great devastations in Ireland and Scotland.

Fig. 30.

KINGS OF TARA OF THE CENÉL nEÓGAIN

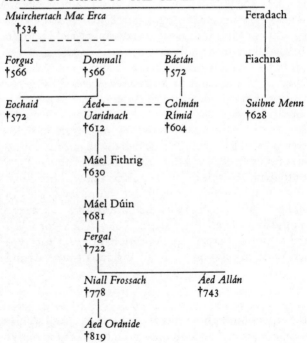

Fig. 31.

KINGS OF TARA OF THE CENÉL CONAILL

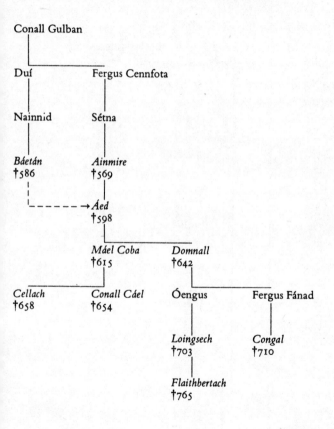

Conall Gulban

Duí — Fergus Cennfota

Nainnid — Sétna

Báetán †586 — *Ainmire* †569

⌞- - - - - →*Áed* †598

Máel Coba †615 — *Domnall* †642

Cellach †658 — *Conall Cáel* †654 — Óengus — Fergus Fánad

Loingsech †703 — *Congal* †710

Flaithbertach †765

Fig. 32.

KINGS OF TARA OF THE SOUTHERN UÍ NÉILL

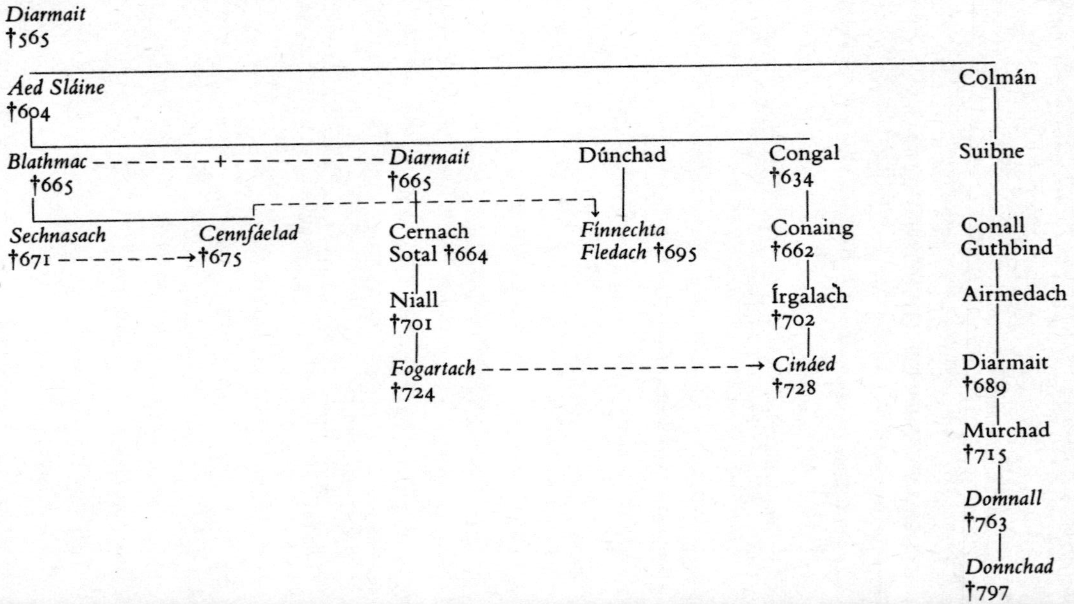

Diarmait
†565

Aed Sláine
†604

Blathmac – – – – + – – – – *Diarmait*
†665   †665

Sechnasach – – – – *Cennfáelad*
†671 – – – –→†675

Cernach
Sotal †664

Niall
†701

Fogartach – – – – – – – – – – –
†724

Dúnchad

Finnechta
Fledach †695

Congal
†634

Conaing
†662

Írgalach
†702

→ *Cináed*
†728

Colmán

Suibne

Conall
Guthbind

Airmedach

Diarmait
†689

Murchad
†715

Domnall
†763

Donnchad
†797

Fig. 33.

RULERS OF ULIDIA: the Dál Fiatach

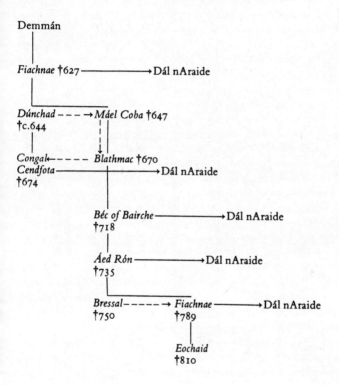

Demmán

Fiachnae †627 ————————→Dál nAraide

Dúnchad – – – →Máel Coba †647
†c.644

Congal←– – – – Blathmac †670
Cendfota ————————→Dál nAraide
†674

Béc of Bairche ————————→Dál nAraide
†718

Áed Rón ————————→Dál nAraide
†735

Bressal – – – – – → Fiachnae ————————→Dál nAraide
†750　　　　　†789

Eochaid
†810

Fig. 34.

RULERS OF ULIDIA: the Dál nAraide

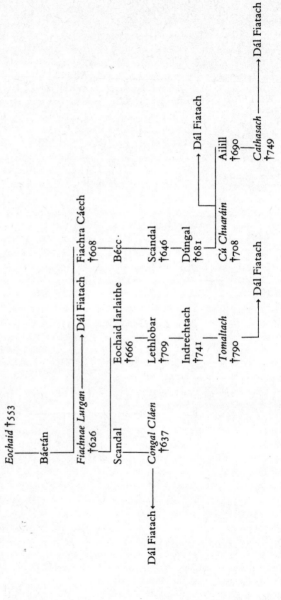

Fig. 35.

RULERS OF CONNACHT: the Uí Briúin

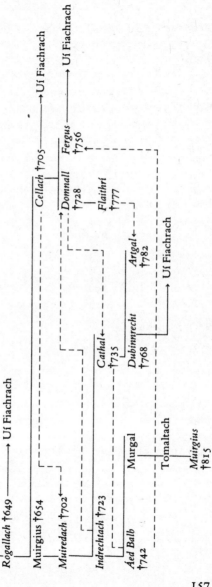

157

Fig. 36.

RULERS OF CONNACHT: the Uí Fiachrach

I. Of the south

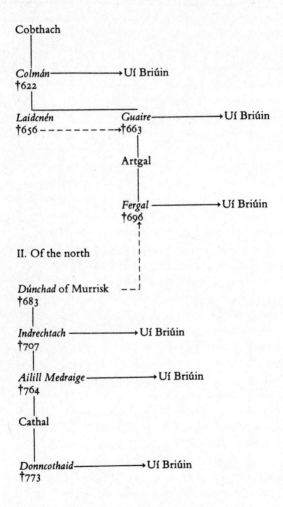

Cobthach

Colmán ⟶ Uí Briúin
†622

Laidcnén   Guaire ⟶ Uí Briúin
†656 - - - - - ⟶ †663

Artgal

Fergal ⟶ Uí Briúin
†696

II. Of the north

Dúnchad of Murrisk - -
†683

Indrechtach ⟶ Uí Briúin
†707

Ailill Medraige ⟶ Uí Briúin
†764

Cathal

Donncothaid ⟶ Uí Briúin
†773

Glossary of Irish Terms

[Note: the definition given applies only to their usage in the text].

aire coisring: the head of a kin-group of commoners, who acts as their representative, and is automatic surety for them in dealings with outside authorities.

aire échta: a commoner charged with an imprecisely defined function in connection with blood-feuds by members of another *tuath* against a member of his own.

aithech fortha: a commoner who acts as defendant on the king's behalf in legal actions against the king.

aithechtuath: an unfree, tribute-paying *tuath*.

aitire: a surety, especially for treaties between *tuath*s, who acts as a kind of hostage in the event of non-fulfilment of obligations.

amnair: a maternal uncle, usually the eldest, who is responsible for a widow and her sons when the latter are not of full age, and her father is dead.

bó-aire: the 'normal' commoner, possessing sufficient land and chattels to make him economically self-sufficient.

bórama: a tribute in cattle, especially the legendary tribute imposed on the Laigin by the Uí Néill.

bothach: a tenant-at-will who receives land and stock from a lord in return for uncertain services.

céle: the client of a lord.

cumal: (1) a female slave; whence (2) the highest unit of

value in ordinary reckoning, usually equivalent to a certain number of milch-cows, varying from time to time; also (3) land of a *cumal*, approximately 35 acres of land, good bad and indifferent.

derbfine: a kin-group comprising all male descendants in the male line of a common great-grandfather.

enech: 'honour', a quality of legal persons defined in terms of so many *séts* (q.v.) or *cumals* (q.v.) according to standing.

feis: the ritual 'mating' of a king with his *tuath*.

fine: the kin-group, the basic unit of society within the *tuath*. See also *derbfine, gelfine, iarfine, indfine*.

fine griain: the kin-group which provides the land for a monastic foundation.

flaith aithig: a commoner with sufficient surplus stock to be able to advance it in fief to other commoners.

fortuath: a *tuath* for whose ruling lineage common descent is not claimed with the ruling dynasty of the province.

fuidir: a tenant-at-will who receives land and stock from a lord in return for uncertain services.

geis (plural *gessa*): a tabu or prohibition, under which certain actions or omissions are expected to prove unfortunate for the person to whom the *geis* is attached.

gelfine: a kin-group comprising all male descendants in the male line of a common grandfather.

iarfine: a kin-group comprising all male descendants in the male line of a common great-great-grandfather.

indfine: a kin-group comprising all male descendants in the male line of a common great-great-great-grandfather.

lánamnas: the bond between husband and wife, father and son, etc.

nemed: a 'sacrosanct' person, one exempt from the ordinary processes of law.

óc-aire: a commoner who, while living on his own land, has not sufficient land and chattels to render him economically self-sufficient.

óenach: an assembly of the people of one or more *tuath*s, convened at regular intervals for athletic and other contests and for the transaction of important public business.

rath: (1) a fief given by a lord to his client (2) also a gift made by an over-king to a subordinate king, also called *cumtach*.

sen-chléithe: a hereditary serf who holds land in return for uncertain services and is alienable as an appurtenance with the land.

sét: a unit of value equivalent to a variable amount of cattle (in one text, *c.* 700, 10 *s.* = 8 milch cows).

tuath: a 'people' whose common bond is rule by a king: the basic political unit in early Irish society.

Bibliography

THE greater part of the political narrative in the preceding pages is of necessity based on the primary sources, that is, the annals transmitted in later compilations such as the *Annals of Ulster*, the *Annals of Innisfallen*, the *Chronicon Scotorum* and the so-called *Annals of Tigernach*. For the period before 800, all derive ultimately from a set of annals kept in the monastery of Iona down to about the third decade of the eighth century, and added to thereafter in a monastery in Meath, probably Clonard. Hence, the affairs of the Uí Néill are what figure most prominently in them, and events in the rest of the country receive only scanty coverage. All sets of annals of course incorporate later interpolations. To the annals an indispensable adjunct, moving sometimes to the level of a political narrative, is the corpus of genealogies and pedigrees of which the core was first compiled, apparently, in the seventh century, and of which a great part was published by M. A. O'Brien, *Corpus Genealogiarum Hiberniae* (Dublin 1962). To this may be added other scattered texts which there is no need to enumerate here.

Of secondary work on political history there is comparatively little. Eóin Mac Néill's *Celtic Ireland* (Dublin 1921) touches partly on this period, and is well worth reading, although unfortunately out of print. To it may be added a series of Thomas Davis Lectures, published under the editorship of M. Dillon under the title, *Early Irish Society* (Dublin 1954), which in some respects brings

Mac Néill up to date. Much of this will be found summarised in L. and M. de Paor, *Early Christian Ireland* (London 1958), with rather more stress on the material culture and art of the period. To these, though less easy reading, should be added Mac Neill's 'Early Irish population groups' *Proceedings of the Royal Irish Academy* XXIX (1911) 59–114.

Among work in the last thirty years, pride of place must be given to T. F. O'Rahilly's *Early Irish History and Mythology* (Dublin 1946, reprinted 1957), less for his positive contributions to the subject (many of which seem to me wrongheaded) than for the admirably destructive criticism there directed against other scholars' views on an enormous range of aspects of the period. O'Rahilly wrote as a philologist rather than as a historian, and the book should be read with O. J. Bergin's criticisms (in *Irish Historical Studies* X, 1956–7, 416–25) in mind; but it has been fertile in so far as it has provoked dissent.

To this may be added a few individual studies: P. Walsh, 'Christian kings of Connacht' *Journal of the Galway Archaeological and Historical Society* XVII, (1937), 124–43, and 'Leinster states and kings in Christian times' *Irish Ecclesiastical Record* LIII, (1939), 47–61; L. Ó Buachalla, 'Contributions towards the political history of Munster, 450–800 A.D.', *Journal of the Cork Historical and Archaeological Society* LVII, (1952), 67–86, LIX, (1954), 111–26, LXI, (1956), 89–102; F. J. Byrne, 'The Ireland of St Columba' *Historical Studies* V (London 1965) 37–58, and *The rise of the Uí Néill and the high-kingship of Ireland* (O'Donnell Lecture, Dublin [1970]); J. Bannerman 'The Dál Riata and Northern Ireland in the sixth and seventh centuries' *Celtic Studies* ed. J. Carney and D. Greene (London 1968) 1–11, and 'Senchus Fer nAlban, Part II' *Celtica* IX, (1971), 217–65; J. V. Kelleher, 'Uí Maine in the annals and genealogies to 1225' *ibid.* 61–112.

On kingship and law, see D. A. Binchy, *Celtic and Anglo-Saxon Kingship* (Oxford 1970) and 'The linguistic and historical value of the Irish law tracts' *Proceedings of the British Academy* XXIX, (1943), and separately. There exists no reliable survey of early Irish law (which in effect means the greater part of early Irish society), although the legal glossary to D. A. Binchy's edition of *Críth Gablach* (Dublin 1941, reprinted 1970), albeit limited to that text, may be found useful. Anyone wishing to go further must make his way through the text-editions by Rudolf Thurneysen and Binchy himself listed in the latter's 'Ancient Irish Law' *Irish Jurist* NS I, (1966), 84–92.

On early Irish economy the only original work available is M. Duignan, 'Irish agriculture in early historic times', *Journal of the Royal Society of Antiquaries of Ireland* LXIV, (1944), 124–43, written largely in protest at some of the more extreme nonsense purveyed in vol. I of the *Cambridge Economic History of Europe*; it may usefully be supplemented by V. B. Proudfoot, 'The economy of the Irish rath' *Medieval Archaeology* VI, (1961), 94–122.

For the church, the literature available is much more plentiful. The polemic centring on the mission of St Patrick is listed in E. Mac Neill, *Saint Patrick* (Dublin 1964) pp. 222–4 – a collection of studies by Mac Neill, of which one, 'The topographical importance of the Vita Tripartita' (pp. 191–220) is of considerable value for early Irish political geography. To this may be added R. P. C. Hanson, *St Patrick: his origins and career* (Oxford 1968), which is particularly useful for a survey of church affairs in Britain at the period. Also useful for the background is K. H. Jackson, *The oldest Irish tradition: a window on the Iron Age* (Cambridge 1964).

On the early Irish church in general, J. F. Kenney's *Sources for the early history of Ireland*, I: Ecclesiastical (New York 1929, reprinted 1966) is always worth reading. J. Ryan, *Irish Monasticism: origins and early development* (Dublin 1931) is still fundamental to its subject; and for an excellent survey, with a good bibliography, see K. Hughes, *The church in early Irish society* (London 1966).

Index

Báegal Bile 46, 84

Báetán son of Cairell, king of Ulidia 74, 77, 78, 87

Báetán son of Muirchertach Mac Erca 72

Báetán son of Nainnid, king of Tara 72, 77, 80

Barrdub daughter of Lethlobar 115

Bé Bail, wife of Cellach of Cualu 110

Bécc son of Cuanu, king of Uí Tuirtri 82, 90

Bécc of Bairrche, king of Ulidia 56, 101, 108, 114, 115

Blathmac son of Áed Sláine, king of Tara 97, 99, 107

Blathmac son of Máel Coba, king of Ulidia 101

Bodbchad of Meath 112

Bran son of Áedán 79

Bran son of Conall, king of Laigin 58, 110

Bran Dub son of Eochu, king of Laigin 44, 81, 82, 84, 90, 91

Bran grandson of Máel Dúin, king of Uí Cinnselaigh 112

Bran Bec son of Murchad, king of Laigin 125, 127

Brénaind son of Muiredach Muinderg 73

Brendan, saint, of Birr 132

Brendan, saint, of Clonfert 24, 132, 148

Bresal Bélach, king of Laigin 15, 16

Bresal son of Áed Rón, king of Ulidia 137

Bríon, ancestor of Uí Briúin 9, 21

Bruide son of Mílchú, king of Picts 75–6

Bruidge, king of Uí Failge 93

Cacht, wife of Muiredach Muillethan 118

Cadoc, saint, of Llangarvan 24

Cainneach, saint, of Aghaboe 86

Cairell, one of three Collas: 13

Cairell son of Muiredach Muinderg, king of Ulidia 73

Cairpre, saint, of Coleraine 24

Cairpre Crom, king of Cashel 86

Cairpre son of Cormac, king of Laigin 19, 26

Cairpre son of Laidcnén, king of Uí Ceinnselaigh 142

Cairpre son of Niall Noígiallach 12, 17

Cairthenn Muach 15

Cathaír Már, ancestor of Laigin 12, 29

Cathal son of Áed 125

Cathal son of Eochaid, king of Uí Crimthainn 143

Cathal son of Finnguine, king of Cashel 121, 123, 124, 130

Cathasach son of Ailill, king of Ulidia 137

Cathasach son or nephew of Etarscél, king of Cashel 130

Cathasach son of Luirgéne, king of Dál nAraide 101

Cathasach son of Máel Dúin, king of Dál nAraide 114

Cathmug grandson of Cellach 135

Cathmug son of Flaithbertach, king of Cairpre 137

Cathnia son of Bécc 130

Cathrannach grandson of Cellach 135

Cathróe, king of Mugdorna 140

Cellach of Cualu, king of Laigin 58, 110, 112, 113

Cellach son of Ailill Molt 86

Cellach son of Dúnchad, king of Laigin 130, 140

Cellach son of Fáelchar, king of Osraige 123, 127, 130

Cellach son of Flann Dá Chongal 130

Cellach son of Máel Coba 97, 98

Cellach son of Rogallach, king of Connacht 118

Cennfáelad, king of Osraige 86

Cennfáelad son of Blathmac, king of Tara 107

Cennfáelad son of Colcu, king of Connacht 100, 115–7

Cennfáelad son of Gerthide 98

Cennfáelad son of Suibne, king of Cianacht 114

Cennselach son of Bran, king of Uí Cheinnselaigh 130

Cernach son of Cathal 125

Cernach son of Diarmait 107

Cerrnceinn 107

Cian, ancestor of Cianacht 4

Ciarán, saint, of Clonmacnois 24, 103, 148

Ciarán, saint, of Seir 24, 84

Cillíne son of Forannán, king of Uí Failge 99

Cináed of Carraig, king of Dál nAraide 139